I0222932

INDIAN WILLS

RECORDS OF THE BUREAU OF INDIAN AFFAIRS

1911 - 1921
BOOK THREE

TRANSCRIBED BY
JEFF BOWEN
NATIVE STUDY
Gallipolis, Ohio
USA

Copyright © 2007
by Jeff Bowen

ALL RIGHTS RESERVED
No part of this publication may be reproduced
or used in any form or manner whatsoever
without previous written permission from the
copyright holder or publisher.

Originally published:
Baltimore, Maryland
2007

Reprinted by:

Native Study LLC
Gallipolis, OH
www.nativestudy.com

Library of Congress Control Number: 2020915163

ISBN: 978-1-64968-028-0

Book cover photograph taken by Jeff Bowen, October, 1998, titled *Early Morning at Fort Toulouse*, where the Coosa and Tallapoosa Rivers meet, Wetumpka, Alabama.

Made in the United States of America.

Other Books and Series by Jeff Bowen

1901-1907 Native American Census Seneca, Eastern Shawnee, Miami, Modoc, Ottawa, Peoria, Quapaw, and Wyandotte Indians (Under Seneca School, Indian Territory)

1932 Census of The Standing Rock Sioux Reservation with Births And Deaths 1924-1932

Census of The Blackfeet, Montana, 1897- 1901 Expanded Edition

Eastern Cherokee by Blood, 1906-1910, Volumes I thru XIII

Choctaw of Mississippi Indian Census 1929-1932 with Births and Deaths 1924-1931   Volume I

Choctaw of Mississippi Indian Census 1933, 1934 & 1937, Supplemental Rolls to 1934 & 1935 with Births and Deaths 1932-1938, and Marriages 1936-1938 Volume II

Eastern Cherokee Census Cherokee, North Carolina 1930-1939 Census 1930-1931 with Births And Deaths 1924-1931 Taken By Agent L. W. Page Volume I

Eastern Cherokee Census Cherokee, North Carolina 1930-1939 Census 1932-1933 with Births And Deaths 1930-1932 Taken By Agent R. L. Spalsbury   Volume II

Eastern Cherokee Census Cherokee, North Carolina 1930-1939 Census 1934-1937 with Births and Deaths 1925-1938 and Marriages 1936 & 1938 Taken by Agents R. L. Spalsbury And Harold W. Foght Volume III

Seminole of Florida Indian Census, 1930-1940 with Birth and Death Records, 1930-1938

Texas Cherokees 1820-1839 A Document For Litigation 1921

Choctaw By Blood Enrollment Cards 1898-1914 Volumes I thru XVII

Starr Roll 1894   (Cherokee Payment Rolls) Districts: Canadian, Cooweescoowee, and Delaware Volume One

Starr Roll 1894 (Cherokee Payment Rolls) Districts: Flint, Going Snake, and Illinois   Volume Two

Starr Roll 1894 (Cherokee Payment Rolls) Districts: Saline, Sequoyah, and Tahlequah; Including Orphan Roll Volume Three

Other Books and Series by Jeff Bowen

Cherokee Intruder Cases Dockets of Hearings 1901-1909 Volumes I & II

Indian Wills, 1911-1921 Records of the Bureau of Indian Affairs
Books One & Two

Visit our website at **www.nativestudy.com** to learn more about these
and other books and series by Jeff Bowen

INTRODUCTION

These documents were found in the *Guide to Records in the National Archives of the United States Relating to AMERICAN INDIANS* on page 98, "eight volumes of copies of Indian wills, 1911-21, that, pursuant to the act of 1910 and an act of February 13, 1913 (37 Stat. 678), were referred to the Bureau and the Office of the Secretary of the Interior for Approval."

The Native American wills and probate records were listed under, "RECORDS OF THE LAW AND PROBATE DIVISIONS." The Law and Probate Divisions evolved from the Land Division that handled legal matters until a separate law office was established in 1907. By 1911, this office was mostly called the Law Division. An act of June 25, 1910 (36 Stat. 855), authorized by the Secretary of the Interior, was to determine the heirs of deceased Indian trust allottees; both the Land Division and the Law Division handled work resulting from this legislation. In 1913, an Heirship Section was established in the land Division that later was mostly concerned with probate work. By 1917, the Division was usually called the Probate Division.

The wills themselves were never filmed until they were discovered by the author and filmed in 1996. The wills and probate records consisted of 2568 pages.

The wills are not numbered in any certain order; there are 181 pages of wills without index in this volume, consisting of approximately 101 different wills. The majority of the wills are of western origin and a few eastern ones that will be reproduced as more volumes are completed.

In *Book Two* there is one will that was actually taken to the highest office in the land, the President of the United States. Also one woman bequeathed to her husband her fishing location and two canoes.

Some of the tribes included among the wills are Sioux, Arickara, Apache, Comanche, Chippewa, Ukie and Wylackie, Omaha, Blackfoot, Squaxin band, Yuma, Cheyenne-Arapahoe, Siletz, Sac and Fox, Quinaielt, Crow, Iowa, Otoe and Missouria, Umatilla, Piegan, Klamath, and many more.

Jeff Bowen
Gallipolis, Ohio
NativeStudy.com

MATILDA WHITTLE

Exhibit "A"

KNOW ALL MEN BY THESE PRESENTS: That I, Matilda Whittle, a resident of Klamath County, State of Oregon, being of sound and disposing mind, and memory, do make, publish and declare this my last will and Testament, in manner and form as follows: that is to say:

FIRST: That all of my just debts, sickness and funeral expenses, be first paid.

SECOND: That I hereby give, devise and bequeath unto my daughter Mrs. M. E. Moreno, all of my property of whatever kind, nature or description, wherever the same may be found or located, consisting either of real estate, personal property, or mixed property, of which I may die seized or possessed. To have and to hold the same absolute and in fee simple.

THIRD: I hereby nominate and appoint, J. W. Siemens, as executor of this my last will and Testament, and request the probate Court, probating this my last Will and Testament, to appoint him without bond.

FOURTH: I hereby revoke all former Wills and Testaments by me made.

IN WITNESS WHEREOF: I, the said Matilda Whittle, have hereunto set my hand and seal to this instrument consisting of one (1) page of typewritten manuscript, on the *21* day of July A. D. 1913, in the City of Klamath Falls, County of Klamath, State of Oregon, in the presence of J. W. Siemens, of Klamath Falls, Oregon, and Bert E. Withrow, of Klamath Falls, Oregon, acquaintances of mine, whom I have requested to become attesting witnesses to this my last Will and Testament.

SIGNED, Sealed and declared in
the presence of us as witnesses.

Matilda Whittle (SEAL)

J. W. Siemens
Bert E Withrow

Probate.
116119-19
221969-19

Department of The Interior,
Office of Indian Affairs, Washington,
JUL 11 1919

The within will of Matilda Whittle, deceased allottee No. 9 on the Klamath Reservation, dated July 21, 1913, is hereby recommended for approval in accordance with the provisions of the Act of June 25, 1910 (36 Stats. L., 855-6) as amended by Act of February 14, 1913 (37 Stats. L., 678), in so far as it involves property held in trust by the Government; but no rights of an executor are recognized in connection with said trust property.

Respectfully,

EB Meritt

Assistant Commissioner

Department of The Interior
Office of The Secretary   JUL 14 1919

The within will of Matilda Whittle, deceased allottee No. 9 on the Klamath Reservation, dated July 21, 1913, is hereby approved in accordance with the Act of June 25, 1910 (36 Stats. L., 855-6) as amended by Act of February 14, 1913 (37 Stats. L., 678), in so far as it involves property held in trust by the Government; but no rights of an executor are recognized in connection with said trust property.

S G Hopkins

Assistant Secretary

WAHPASSET WHIZ

OFFICE OF INDIAN AFFAIRS
RECEIVED
FEB 23 1918
15933

LAST WILL AND TESTAMENT
OF WAHPASSET WHIZ.

IN THE NAME OF GOD, AMEN.

I, Wahpasset Whiz, of Yakima County, Washington, being of sound and disposing mind, memory and understanding, considering the certainty of death and the uncertainty of the time thereof, and being desirous to settle my worldly affairs, and thereby be the better prepared to leave this worldwhen it shall please the Almighty to call me hence, do therefore make and publish this my last Will and Testament, hereby revoking and annulling all wills by me heretofore made, in manner and form following, that is to say:

FIRST, and principally, I commit my soul into the hands of Almighty God, and my body to the earth, to be decently buried: and my Will is, that all my just debts and funeral expenses shall be paid as soon after my decease as may be convenient;

SECOND, I give, devise, and bequeath to my beloved wife, Nellie Whiz, and to her heirs and assigns forever, all the property, both real, personal, and mixed, that I may now own or that I may afterwards possess.

THIRD, to my half sister, Annie Riddle, I bequeath the sum of Five Dollars ($5.00).

All the rest and residue of my estate, both real, personal and mixed, I give, devise and bequeath to my beloved wife, Hollie Whiz, as aforesaid, and to her heirs and assigns forever.

IN TESTIMONY WHEREOF, I have set my hand and seal to this, my last Will and Testament, at Fort Simcoe, Yakima County, Washington, this 19th day of July, in the year of our Lord, one thousand nine hundred and sixteen.

Wahpasset Whiz.
His [thumb print] Mark.
(Seal)

SIGNED, SEALED, PUBLISHED, AND DECLARED, by WAHpasset[sic] Whiz, the above-named testator, as and for his last Will and Testament, in our presence, and at his request, and in his presence, and in the presence of each other, we have hereunto subscribed our names as attesting witnesses.

Stuart H. Elbott
Residence Ft Simcoe, Wash

Abraham Lincoln
Residence Ft Simcoe, Wash.

Probate.
15834-18
15933-18
J W H

Department of The Interior,
Office of Indian Affairs, Washington,
JUL -9 1919

The within will of Wahpasset Whiz, Deceased Yakima allottee No. 1826, is hereby recommended for approval in accordance with the provisions of the Act of June 25, 1910 (36 Stats. L., 855-6) as amended by Act of February 14, 1913 (37 Stats. L., 678)..

Respectfully,
EB Meritt
Assistant Commissioner

Department of The Interior
Office of The Secretary   JUL 15 1919

The within will of Wahpasset Whiz, Deceased Yakima allottee No. 1826, is hereby approved in accordance with the Act of June 25, 1910 (36 Stats. L., 855-6) as amended by Act of February 14, 1913 (37 Stats. L., 678)..

S G Hopkins
Assistant Secretary

▲▼▲▼▲▼▲▼▲▼▲▼▲▼▲▼

BIG SNAKE

Last Will and Testament
of
Big Snake

IN THE NAME OF GOD, AMEN.

I, *Big Snake* of *St Xavier, Mont* being of sound mind, memory, and understanding, do hereby make and publish this my last will and testament, hereby revoking and annulling all wills by me heretofore made, in manner and form following, that is to say:

First; I direct that all my just debts and funeral expenses, and expenses of my last illness shall be paid by my executor hereinafter named as soon after my decease as convenient;

4

Second; I give, devise and bequeath to

One Star all of my property both personal and real.

Third; All the rest and residue of my estate, both real, and personal and mixed, I give devise and bequeath to my lawful heirs as determined after my decease.

And lastly; I do hereby nominate, constitute and **appoint** *Supt Crow Agency Mont* executor of this my last will and testament.

In testimony Whereof, I have set my hand and seal to this, my last will and Testament, at *St. Xavier* Montana, this *fourth* day of *April*, in the year of our Lord one thousand nine hundred and *seventeen.*   *His*

Big Snake [thumb print]

mark.

Signed, sealed, published and declared by said *Big Snake* in our presence, as and for *his* last Will and testament, and at *his* request and in our presence, and in the presence of each other, we have hereunto subscribed our names as attesting witnesses thereto.

D.E. McDaniel	of	*St. Xavier, Montana*
Carl Crooked Arm	of	*St. Xavier, Montana*

Department of The Interior,
Office of Indian Affairs, Washington,
JUL 7 1919

It is recommended that the within will be approved pursuant to the provisions of the Act of June 25, 1910 (36 Stats. L., 855-6) as amended by Act of February 14, 1913 (37 Stats. L., 678).

Respectfully,

EB Meritt

Assistant Commissioner

Department of The Interior
Office of The Secretary

The within will is approved pursuant to the provisions of the Act of June 25, 1910 (36 Stats. L., 855-6) as amended by Act of February 14, 1913 (37 Stats. L., 678).

S G Hopkins

Assistant Secretary

▲▼▲▼▲▼▲▼▲▼▲▼▲▼▲▼

MRS. WALPASSI or MRS. LOWLACE or KU-MUSH-NAI

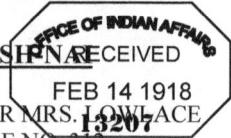

OFFICE OF INDIAN AFFAIRS
RECEIVED
FEB 14 1918
13207

LAST WILL AND TESTAMENT OF MRS. WALPASSI, OR MRS. LOWLACE
OR KU MUSH NAI, WARM SPRING ALLOTTEE NO. 312

I, Mrs. Walpassi or Mrs. Lowlace or Ku-mush-nai, age 80 years and a full blood indian[sic] of the Warm Spring Reservation in Oregon, being allottee No. 312 of that place and being of sound mind and disposing memory and acting under no undue influence, duress or suggestion from any person, do hereby make this my last will and testament and expressly revoke all former wills by me heretofore made.

FIRST, I devise that all just debts and funeral expenses be paid and that a suitable monument be erected over my grave.

SECOND, I give devise and bequeth unto my grandson Joe McCorkle, age 27 years, all of my property, both real and personal and mixed which I now possess or may afterwards acquire. My real property consists, as far as I know, of my own allotment upon the Warm Spring Reservation, No. 312, which is described as follows:

W/2 SE/4	Sec. 33 T 7 R 11
W/2 Lots 22 & 27	Sec. 33 T 9 R 12
Lot 1	Sec. 1 T 8 R 10 116.83 Acres.

and also the property of my previously deceased husband, Wal-passi or Tichmonan, who was Warm Spring allottee No. 311 and whose allotment is described as follows:

SW/4 Sec. 33 T 7 R 11   160 Acres.

(Heirs determined under file L.H. 33722-1916 J G McG). My husband also inherits 40 acres of land upon the Yakima Reservation, Washington. This being the allotment of Charley Yethowat. I do not know either the number or the description of the land on the Yakima Reservation.

THIRD, I give, devise and bequeth all of my personal property consisting of any horses and money which I may have at the time of my death, unto my grandson, as aforesaid, Joe McCorkle.

6

FOURTH, All of the rest and residue of the property which I may now have or possess I give, devise and bequeth to my grandson, as aforesaid, Joe McCorkle.

FIFTH, I am aware of the fact that my natural heirs would be Warren McCorkle, my son, Joe McCorkle, my grandson and Thomas Wainanwit, my grandson, but I expressly make this will with the view of disinheriting Thomas Wainanwit and Warren McCorkle for the reasons that Warren McCorkle, my son, has received his share of my property a number of years ago in a gift of cattle which I had, and other property and, further, for the reason that neither my son Warren McCorkle or grandson Thomas Wainanwit has ever done anything for me but that my grandson Joe McCorkle has tenderly cared for me in sickness and health and has always been ready to aid me in any way.

Signed this 8th day of January 1918.

WITNESSES TO MARK:

Georgiana Meachem   Her   [thumb print] Mark.
A M Reynolds   Mrs. Walpassi, Ku mush nai,
                              or Mrs. Lowlace

I, Georgiana Meachem and A.M. Reynolds do hereby state that we have seen the above named testator place her thumbmark to this, her last will and testament and that we do hereby affix our names as witnesses to the last will and testament of Mrs. Walpassi at her request and in her presence and in the presence of each other.

> *Georgiana Meachem*
> Attesting Witness.
> *A M Reynolds*
> Attesting Witness.

I, Georgiana Meachem, of legal age and a resident of Warmspring, Oregon do hereby certify that I have duly interpreted the contents of this will to the above named Testator Mrs. Walpassi to the best of my ability and that she has stated to me that she understands all the provisions contained therein.

> *Georgiana Meachem*
> Interpreter.

Indian Wills, 1911 – 1921 Book Three
Records of The Bureau of Indian Affairs

Probate
82387-18

Department of The Interior,
Office of Indian Affairs, Washington,
JUL 11 1919
The last will and testament of Mrs. Walpassie or Lowlace or Ku-much-
nai, deceased allottee No. 312 on the Warm Springs Reservation in
Oregon, which will was executed on January 8, 1918, is hereby
recommended for approval according to the Acts of June 25, 1910 (36
Stat. L., 855-6), and February 14, 1913 (37 Stat. L., 678).

Respectfully,
EB Meritt
Assistant Commissioner

Department of The Interior
Office of The Secretary JUL 14 1919

The last will and testament of Mrs. Walpassie or Lowlace or Ku-much-
nai, deceased allottee No. 312 on the Warm Springs Reservation in
Oregon, which will was executed on January 8, 1918, is hereby
recommended for approval according to the Acts of June 25, 1910 (36
Stat. L., 855-6), and February 14, 1913 (37 Stat. L., 678).

SG Hopkins
Assistant Secretary

▲▼▲▼▲▼▲▼▲▼▲▼▲▼
CATHERINE MITCHELL

LAST WILL AND TESTAMENT
of
CATHERINE MITCHELL

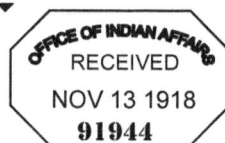

OFFICE OF INDIAN AFFAIRS
RECEIVED
NOV 13 1918
91944

I, Catherine Mitchell, of Tacoma, Pierce County, Wash., being
of sound and disposing mind and memory, do hereby make, publish and
declare this to be my last will and testament, hereby revoking any and all
former wills by me at any time heretofore made.

FIRST: It is my desire that my executor, herein after named,

8

shall as soon as he has sufficient funds in his hands, pay all just charges for administration and funeral expenses.

SECOND: I hereby devise and bequeath to each of my children who survive me, the following, to-wit: To Lillie Tittle, I give my silver set, also my upholstered parlor set; to Lizzie LeClaire, I give my silver knives and forks; to Emily Hunt, I give the picture of her father, Theo. Gard; to Nettie Varner, I give my own picture and the picture o my mother; and to Laura Varner, I give my moon stone earrings.

THIRD: To Nellie Perkins, I give and bequeath my watch and chain and my sewing machine.

FOURTH: I direct that all interest I have in Lots Eight (8), eleven (11) and twelve (12), in Block Eight Thousand Three Hundred Fifty-seven (8357) in the Indian Addition to the City of Tacoma, shall be sold by my executor hereinafter named, as soon as he can obtain a price therefore which in his judgment is fair and reasonable, and convert the same into cash; that from the proceeds of said sale, the expenses of my last sickness and funeral shall be paid, and if there be any surplus remaining that such surplus money be equally divided amongst all of my daughters who survive me.

FIFTH: My allotment on the Yakima Reservation, Wash., I give, devise and bequeath to my husband, John Mitchell, my daughters, Laura Varner; Nettie Varner; Emily Hunt; Lizzie LeClaire and Lillie Tittle, and to Nellie Perkins, or to such of them as survive me, in equal shares.

SIXTH: Any and all other estate of which I die seized or have any interest in, I give, devise and bequeath to my husband John Mitchell.

SEVENTH: Should my husband, John Mitchell, die before my own death then and in that event, I give, devise and bequeath to my daughters who survive me and to Nellie Perkins, share and share alike, all my estate of which I may die seized or have any interest in whatsoever.

EIGHTH: I hereby constitute and appoint my said husband, John Mitchell, the executor of this my last will and testament, and I hereby give to him full power to grant, bargain, sell and convey any and all of my property and estate, whether it be real, personal or mixed and empower him to take possession and control thereof; and I further direct that no bond be required of him as executor of this will and that after the proving of this will he shall settle my said estate without the intervention of any court.

In Witness Whereof, I hereunto set my hand and seal this *12* day of January, A.D., 1913.

her

Catherine X Mitchell

mark

The foregoing writing was signed, sealed, published and declared by the above named Catherine Mitchell as and for her last will and testament in the presence of us, who at her request and in her presence and in the presence of each other, have subscribed our names as attesting witnesses thereto this *12* day of January, A.D., 1913.

> *Ida McQuesten*
> Residing at Tacoma, Washington.
> *G. Dows McQuesten*
> Residing at Tacoma, Washington.

I certify that I signed the testator's name in her presence and at her request, -she signing by "x-mark"

> *G. Dows McQuesten*

Department of The Interior,
Office of Indian Affairs, Washington,
JUL 9 1919
The foregoing will of Catherine Mitchell, Yakima allottee No. 3965, so far as it applies to her trust property is recommended for approval in accordance with the Act of June 25, 1910 (36 Stats. L., 855-6) as amended by Act of February 14, 1913 (37 Stats. L., 678).

> Respectfully,
> *EB Meritt*
> Assistant Commissioner

Department of The Interior
Office of The Secretary
JUL 15 1919

The foregoing will of Catherine Mitchell, Yakima allottee No. 3965, so far as it applies to her trust property is recommended for approval in accordance with the Act of June 25, 1910 (36 Stats. L., 855-6) as amended by Act of February 14, 1913 (37 Stats. L., 678).

S G Hopkins
Assistant Secretary

▲ ▼ ▲ ▼ ▲ ▼ ▲ ▼ ▲ ▼ ▲ ▼ ▲ ▼ ▲ ▼

PEOPEOTOWEASH

LAST WILL AND TESTAMENT

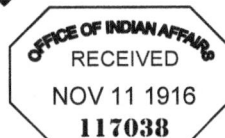

> OFFICE OF INDIAN AFFAIRS
> RECEIVED
> NOV 11 1916
> 117038

IN THE NAME OF GOD, AMEN.

I, Peopeotoweash, Cayuse allottee No. 155, of the Umatilla Indian reservation, being of sound mind, memory and understanding, do hereby make and publish this my last will and testament, hereby revoking and annulling all wills by me heretofore made, in manner and form following, that is to say:

First: I direct that all my just debts and funeral expenses, and expenses of my last illness, shall be paid as soon after my decease as shall be convenient:

Second: I give, devise and bequeath to my wife, Ipnametoyket, my son, Leo Sampson, and my grandson, John Sampson, 40 acres of my allotment, together with improvements thereon, described as NW/4 SE/4, Sec. 28, T. 2 N, R 33, E., W.M. To my grandson, John Sampson, I give 40 acres of my allotment described as the SE/4-NW/4 Sec. 26, T. 2 In, R. 33 E., W.M.; and to my son Leo Sampson I give the remainder of my allotment described as the N/2 NW/4 Sec. 26, T.2 N., R. 33, E., W.M., all in Oregon.

IN TESTIMONY WHEREOF, I have set my hand and seal to this my last will and testament, at Umatilla Indian Agency, this **thirtieth** day of **October**, in the year of our Lord, One Thousand, Nine Hundred and Sixteen.

His
Peopeotoweash   [thumb print]
mark.

Sign, sealed, published and declared by the said Peopeotoweash in our presence as and for **his** last will and testament, and at **his** request and in our presence, and in the presence of each other, we have hereunto subscribed our names as attesting witnesses thereto.

Mitchell Lloyd
John V (Illegible)
Mary T Sampson
(Name Illegible)
All of Pludleton Oregon

▲▼▲▼▲▼▲▼▲▼▲▼▲

OFFICE OF INDIAN AFFAIRS
RECEIVED
OCT 13 1916
107401

EMILY BELLE LEWIS

LAST WILL AND TESTIMENT[sic] OF EMILEY BELLE LEWIS.

In the name of God, amen, I, Emiley Belle Lewis, of lawful age, and of sound mind and disposing memory, realizing the uncertainty of life and the certainty of death, do make, ordain, publish and declare this my last will and testiment[sic], hereby revoking all other or former wills, heretofore made by me.

Item One. I direct that out of my estate all of my just debts and funeral expenses be first paid; and that a suitable monument, costing not to exceed Five Hundred ($500.00) be erected at my grave.

Item Two. I give, devise, and bequeath all the rest, residue and remainder of my estate, wheresoever the same may be situated, to my children and grand-child, to be divided equally between them, share and share alike as follows:

(a) My daythter[sic], Louisa Victoria Hardy, of Burbank, Oklahoma, an equal undivided one-fifth in the remaining two-thirds of my estate;

(b) Julia Goldie Clark, my daughter, of Burbank, Okla. an equal undivided one-fifth in the remaining two-thirds of my estate.

(c) Geneva Hardy, my daughter of Burbank, Oklahoma, an equal undivided one-fifth in the remaining two-thirds of my estate.

(d) William Ray Hardy, my son of Hardy, Okla, an equal undivided one-fifth interest in the remaining two-thirds of my estate.

(e) Kenneth Clark, my grand-child, an equal undivided one-fifth interest in the remaining two-thirds of my estate.

Said children and said grand-child to share and share alike the said remaining two-thirds of my estate.

In case any of the said children or the said grand-child should die prior to my death, then the said remaining two-thirds of my estate shall be divided equally share and share alike, among the survivors.

Item Five. It is my will that my homestead, which is included in the above will and testiment[sic], shall not be sold or encumbered until each one of the Devisees herein shall have reached his or her majority; and that then said homestead may be sold and the proceeds divided as herein provided, in the meantime the income from said homestead shall be divided according to the terms of this will, among the Devisees herein.

Item Six. It is my will and desire that my former husband, William Hardy, of Hardy, Oklahoma, be given the custody and care of our children, Julia Goldie Clark, Geneva Hardy, and William Ray Hardy.

Item Seven. I hereby nominate, constitute and appoint the said William Hardy, my former husband, as the executor of this my last will and testiment[sic]

In witness whereof, I have hereunto set my hand this *22* day of July, 1916, at Arkansas City, Kansas, in the presence of the subscribing witnesses, who in my presence and in the presence of each other, have hereunto set their names as subscribing witnesses.

Emily Lewis

We, the undersigned subscribing witnesses to the above will, do hereby certify that the above named testator published and declared the above will to be her last will and testiment[sic] in our presence, and signed the same in our presence, who at her request, in her presence and the presence of each other have hereunto subscribed our names, this *22* day of July, 1916, at Arkansas City, Kansas.

Maxine Collins
Pansy Akin

13

Indian Wills, 1911 – 1921 Book Three
Records of The Bureau of Indian Affairs

I, Charley Lewis, Burbank, Oklahoma, the husband of the above named testatrix, having read over and fully understanding the above will, do hereby consent to the making of the said will by said testatrix and consent to all the terms and provisions thereof, and hereby consent to the enforcement thereof.

In witness whereof, I have hereunto set my hand this *22* day of July, 1916 at Arkansas City, Kansas, in the presence of the subscribing witnesses, who in my presence and in the presence of each other have hereunto set their names as witnesses to my consent to the above will.

Have Charley Lewis sign here }   *Chas L Lewis*

We, the undersigned, subscribing witnesses to the above and foregoing will, hereby certify the above will and the contents thereto were read over to and by the above names Charley Lewis in our presence and that he subscribed the same and gave his consent thereto in our presence, at his requests, in his presence and the presence of each other, have hereunto set our names as subscribing witnesses at Arkansas City, Kansas, this *22* day of July, 1916.

Maxine Collins
Pansy Akin

Law-Heirship
10740-16
F.E.

Department of The Interior,
Office of Indian Affairs, Washington,
FEB -2 1917
It is recommended that the within will of Emily Belle Lewis (Emily Hardy) be approved in pursuance with the Act of June 25, 1910 (36 Stats. L., 855-6) as amended by Act of February 14, 1913 (37 Stats. L., 678), so far as her homestead and trust property is involved.

Respectfully,
EB Meritt
Assistant Commissioner
Department of The Interior
Office of The Secretary FEB 10 1917

The within will of Emily Belle Lewis is approved in pursuance with the Act of June 25, 1910 (36 Stats. L., 855-6) as amended by Act of February 14, 1913 (37 Stats. L., 678), so far as her homestead and trust property is involved..

Bo Sweeney
Assistant Secretary

Recorded 3/29/17 FE

▲▼▲▼▲▼▲▼▲▼▲▼▲▼▲▼

MOSES BOYDE

*I, **Moses Boyde** of (Blank) in the County of **Redwood** and State of **Minnesota** being of sound mind and memory, do make, ordain, publish and declare this to be my last Will and Testament.*

FIRST, I order and direct that my Executrix hereinafter named pay all my just debts and funeral expenses as soon after my decease as conveniently may be.

*SECOND, After the payment of such funeral expenses and debts, I give, devise and bequeath unto my wife **Mamie Boyde for herself and my daughter Mary Boyde** all the property, real and personal, and effects of every name and nature which I now have, may die possessed of, or may be entitled to, her heirs and assigns forever.*

*THIRD, I do by this, my Will, dispose of the custody and tuition of my Children, who shall be minors at and after my decease, during their minority, to my wife **Mamie Boyde** and do hereby appoint her their Guardian.*

*FOURTH, I do hereby make, constitute and appoint my wife **Mamie Boyde** sole Executrix of this, my Last Will and Testament, and it is my wish, and I do hereby request, that she may not be compelled to give any bond or security as such Executrix, or as Guardian, and that she may settle the estate in her own way and sell any or all of the real or personal estate, at public or private sale, as she may think best, and pay the debts without being compelled to account to the Probate or any other Court; and I do hereby revoke all and every former Will by me made.*

𝔍𝔫 𝔗𝔢𝔰𝔱𝔦𝔪𝔬𝔫𝔶 𝔚𝔥𝔢𝔯𝔢𝔬𝔣, *I have hereunto subscribed my name and affixed my seal this **20th** day of **February** in the year of our Lord one thousand nine hundred and **Seventeen**.*

Moses Boyde (Seal)

𝔗𝔥𝔦𝔰 𝔍𝔫𝔰𝔱𝔯𝔲𝔪𝔢𝔫𝔱 *was, on the day of the date thereof, signed, published and declared by the said testator **Moses Boyde** to be his Last Will and Testament, in our presence, who, at his request, have subscribed our names thereto as witnesses, in his presence and in the presence of each other.*

Henry Fishit	*residing at*	**Morton, Minn.**
F.E. Sylvester	*residing at*	**Morton, Minn.**

Probate
20230-1917,
R T B

Department of The Interior,
Office of Indian Affairs, Washington,

It is recommended that the within will of Moses Boyde of the Santee Tribe, unallotted but having trust personalty[sic] and late of Pipestone be approved in accordance with the Act of June 25, 1910 (36 Stats. L., 855-6) as amended by Act of February 14, 1913 (37 Stats. L., 678), but no appointment of an executrix can be recognized.

Respectfully,
EB Meritt
Assistant Commissioner

Department of The Interior
Office of The Secretary SEP 25 1917

The within will of Moses Boyde of the Santee Tribe, unallotted but having trust property, late of Pipestone be approved in accordance with the Act of June 25, 1910 (36 Stats. L., 855-6) as amended by Act of February 14, 1913 (37 Stats. L., 678), but no appointment of an executrix can be recognized.

SG Hopkins
Assistant Secretary

▲ ▼ ▲ ▼ ▲ ▼ ▲ ▼ ▲ ▼ ▲ ▼ ▲ ▼ ▲ ▼

Indian Wills, 1911 – 1921 Book Three
Records of The Bureau of Indian Affairs

<u>IRON BEAR</u>

Original WILL

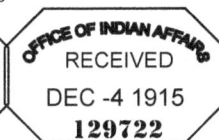

OFFICE OF INDIAN AFFAIRS
RECEIVED
MAR 18 1916
30016

OFFICE OF INDIAN AFFAIRS
RECEIVED
DEC -4 1915
129722

I, **Iron Bear** of Pine Ridge Agency, South Dakota, Allottee number **1979** do hereby make and declare this to be my last will and testament, in accordance with Section 2 of the Act of June 25, 1910, (36 stat. 855-858) and Act of February 14, 1913, (Public No. 381), hereby revoking all former wills made by me:

1. I hereby direct that as soon as possible after my decease, that all my debts, funeral and testamentary expenses be paid out of my personal estate.

2. I give and devise my allotment on the Pine Ridge Reservation, South Dakota, described as follows:

All of Section 26 in Township 40 north of Ranged 38 west of the Sixth Principal Meridian, South Dakota, containing 640 acres.

in the following manner:

> **To my son, Alec Iron Bear: the SE/4 of Sec. 26 in Twp. 40 N. of Range 38 W.**
> **To my son, James Iron Bear: the NE/4 of Sec. 26 in Twp. 40 N. of Range 38 W.**
> **To my son, Fred Iron Bear: the NW/4 of Sec. 26 in Twp. 40 N. of Range 38 W.**
> **The SW/4 of Sec. 26 in T. 40 N. of Range 38, I wish to sell and the proceeds to be used for the support of myself and wife, Julia Iron Bear. If any of the proceeds remain to go to my wife and if this quarter section does not sell, to be given my wife.**

3. I give and bequeath all of my personal property of whatsoever nature and wheresoever situated unto

> **my wife, Julia Iron Bear.**

4. All the rest of my property, real or personal, now possessed or hereafter acquired, of whatsoever nature and wheresoever situated, I hereby give, devise and bequeath unto

17

my son, Alec Iron Bear, and my nephew, James White Deer, in equal shares.

In witness whereof I have hereunto set my hand this **20th** day of **October** 1915.

his
mark   [thumb print]

Iron Bear

      The above statement was, this **20th** day of **October** 1915 signed and published by **Iron Bear** as **his** last will and testament, in the joint presence of the undersigned, the said **Iron Bear** then being of sound and vigorous mid and free from any constraint or compulsion; whereupon we, being without any interest in the matter other than friendship, and being well acquainted with **him** but not members of **his** family, immediately subscribed our names hereto in the presence of each other and of the said testator, for the purpose of attesting the said will, as **he** requested us to do. And that I, **George A. Trotter** at the testator.'s request have written ……. name in ink, and that **he** affixed **his** thumb-marks.

<table>
<tr><td></td><td>Post Office Address</td></tr>
<tr><td>*George A Trotter*</td><td>**Pine Ridge, S. D.**</td></tr>
<tr><td>*Frank C. Goings*</td><td>**Pine Ridge, S. D.**</td></tr>
</table>

Pine Ridge, South Dakota.
NOV 29 1915

      I hereby certify that I have fully inquired into the mental competency of the Indian signing the above will; the circumstances attending the execution of the will; the influence that may have induced its execution, and the names of those entitled to share in the estate under the law of descent in South Dakota: reasons for the disposition of the property proposed by the will differing from disposition had the property descended by operation of law.

      I respectfully forward this will with the recommendation that it be …..approved.

John R Brennan
Supt. & Spl. Disb. Agent.

(Second will of Iron Bear below)

18

Original
WILL

OFFICE OF INDIAN AFFAIRS
RECEIVED
MAR 18 1916
30016

I, **Iron Bear** of Pine Ridge Agency, South Dakota, Allottee number **1979** do hereby make and declare this to be my last will and testament, in accordance with Section 2 of the Act of June 25, 1910, (36 stat. 855-858) and Act of February 14, 1913, (Public No. 381), hereby revoking all former wills made by me:

1. I hereby direct that as soon as possible after my decease, that all my debts, funeral and testamentary expenses be paid out of my personal estate.

2. I give and devise interest in the allotment of Comes In Sight, Pine Ridge Sioux allottee No. 4922, described as follows:

SW/4 of Sec. 10, T. 39 N., R. 35 w. of the 6th P.M. in S.D., containing 160 acres.

Also any other real or personal property I may hereafter acquire, of whatsoever nature.

in the following manner:

To my wife and children equally

All other property belonging to me to be devised as set out in my previous will dated October 20, 1915.

In witness whereof I have hereunto set my hand this ***ninth*** day of ***March*** 1916.

his
Iron Bear   [thumb print]
mark

The above statement was, this ***9th*** day of ***March*** 191***6,*** signed and published by **Iron Bear** as **his** last will and testament, in the joint presence of the undersigned, the said **Iron Bear** then being of sound and vigorous mid and free from any constraint or compulsion; whereupon we, being without any interest in the matter other than friendship, and being well acquainted with **him** but not members of **his** family, immediately subscribed our names hereto in the presence of each other and of the said

Indian Wills, 1911 – 1921 Book Three
Records of The Bureau of Indian Affairs

testator, for the purpose of attesting the said will, as **he** requested us to do. And that I, *Elmer B Pomeroy* at the testator.'s request have written **his** name in ink, and that **he** affixed *his* thumb-mark.

<table>
<tr><td></td><td>Post Office Address</td></tr>
<tr><td>*Elmer B Pomeroy   Farmer*</td><td>*Wanblee, S.D.*</td></tr>
<tr><td>*Noah Bad Wound*</td><td>*Wanblee, S.D.*</td></tr>
</table>

Pine Ridge, South Dakota.
MAR 13 1916

I hereby certify that I have fully inquired into the mental competency of the Indian signing the above will; the circumstances attending the execution of the will; the influence that may have induced its execution, and the names of those entitled to share in the estate under the law of descent in South Dakota: reasons for the disposition of the property proposed by the will differing from disposition had the property descended by operation of law.

I respectfully forward this will with the recommendation that it be …..approved.

John R Brennan
Supt. & Spl. Disb. Agent.

Department of The Interior,
Office of Indian Affairs, Washington,
SEP -6 1916

It is recommended that the within will dated October 20, 1915, and the codicil dated March 9, 1916, be approved in accordance with the Act of June 25, 1910 (36 Stats. L., 855-6) as amended by Act of February 14, 1913 (37 Stats. L., 678).

Respectfully,
EB Meritt
Assistant Commissioner

Department of The Interior
Office of The Secretary   SEP 14 1916

The within will dated October 20, 1915, and the codicil dated March 9, 1916, are hereby approved in accordance with the Act of June 25, 1910 (36 Stats. L., 855-6) as amended by Act of February 14, 1913 (37 Stats. L., 678).

Bo Sweeney
Assistant Secretary

▲▼▲▼▲▼▲▼▲▼▲▼▲▼▲▼

Indian Wills, 1911 – 1921 Book Three
Records of The Bureau of Indian Affairs

LEGGINS DOWN
WILL.

I, Leggins Down of Pine Ridge Agency, South Dakota, Allottee number 4287 do hereby make and declare this to be my last will and testament, in accordance with Section 2 of the Act of June 25, 1910, (36 stat. 855-858) and Act of February 14, 1913, (Public No. 381), hereby revoking all former wills made by me:

1. I hereby direct that as soon as possible after my decease, that all my debts, funeral and testamentary expenses be paid out of my personal estate.

2. I give and devise my allotment on the Pine Ridge Reservation, South Dakota, described as follows:

the north half of Section 10 in Township 40 north of Range 35 west of the Sixth Principal Meridian, South Dakota, containing 320 acres,

in the following manner:

To my nephew, William McGaa, Sr.

3. I give and bequeath all of my personal property of whatsoever nature and wheresoever situated unto my nephew, William McGaa, Sr.

4. All the rest of my property, real or personal, now possessed or hereafter acquired, of whatsoever nature and wheresoever situated, I hereby give, devise and bequeath unto my nephew, William McGaa, Sr.

In witness whereof I have hereunto set my hand this 28th day of September 1915.

LEGGINS DOWN.   (Her thumb mark).

The above statement was, this 28th day of September 1915 signed and published by Leggins Down as her last will and testament, in the joint presence of the undersigned, the said Leggins Down then being of sound and vigorous mid and free from any constraint or compulsion; whereupon we, being without any interest in the matter other than friendship, and being well acquainted with her but not members of her family, immediately subscribed our names hereto in the presence of each other and of the said testator, for the purpose of attesting the said will, as she requested us to do. And that I, George A. Trotter at the testatrix.'s request have written her name in ink, and that she affixed her thumb-mark.

	Post Office Address
(Signed) GEORGE A. TROTTER	Kyle, South Dakota.
(Signed) JOHN ROCK	Porcupine, South Dakota.

Pine Ridge, South Dakota.
Nov 8 - 1915

I hereby certify that I have fully inquired into the mental competency of the Indian signing the above will; the circumstances attending the execution of the will; the influence that may have induced its execution, and the names of those entitled to share in the estate under the law of descent in South Dakota: reasons for the disposition of the property proposed by the will differing from disposition had the property descended by operation of law.

I respectfully forward this will with the recommendation that it be approved.

(Signed) JOHN R BRENNAN,
Supt. & Spl. Disb. Agent.

I, Leggins Down, of lawful age, having on September 28, 1915, made and executed a will in favor of William McGaa, Sr., desire now to modify the same in so far as it applies to any property I may hereinafter acquire by will, or otherwise, devising the same, if any there be, to my natural heirs at law instead of to William McGaa. Sr.

Further I sayeth nothing.

her
(Signed) LEGGINS DOWN   thumb
mark.

Subscribed to in our presence this 28 day of March, Nineteen hundred and sixteen.

(Signed) CHAS. D. PARKHURST.
(Signed) JOHN ROCK.

Department of The Interior,
Office of Indian Affairs, Washington,

SEP 2 - 1916

It is recommended that the within will of Leggins Down, Pine Ridge Allottee No. 4287 dated September 28, 1915, and the codicil dated March 28, 1916, be approved under the Act of June 25, 1910 (36 Stats. L., 855-6) as amended by Act of February 14, 1913 (37 Stats. L., 678).

Respectfully,

(Signed)   EB MERITT

Assistant Commissioner.

Department of The Interior

Office of The Secretary   SEP 7 1916

The within will of Leggins Down, Pine Ridge Allottee No. 4287 dated September 28, 1915, and the codicil dated March 28, 1916, are hereby approved in accordance with the Act of June 25, 1910 (36 Stats. L., 855-6) as amended by Act of February 14, 1913 (37 Stats. L., 678).

(Signed)   BO SWEENEY

Assistant Secretary

▲▼▲▼▲▼▲▼▲▼▲▼▲▼▲▼

MADELINE STEPHAN

COPY OF WILL.

LAST WILL AND TESTAMENT.

IN THE NAME OF GOD, AMEN:

I, Madeline Stephan, now residing at Chautauqua, in the State of Kansas, realizing the uncertainty of life and the certainty of death, and being of sound and disposing mind and memory do hereby make, publish and declare this to be my LAST WILL AND TESTAMENT hereby revoking all former Wills by me made:

1. I hereby direct that all of my just debts and funeral expenses be paid as soon after my death as may be convenient to my Executor.

2. I hereby give, devise and bequeath unto my beloved husband, William A. Stephan, all of my property, real, personal and mixed to be his forever.

3.   In the event that I should survive my husband, William A. Stephan, all of my property both real, personal and mixed, I hereby give, devise and bequeath unto my friend, Miss Celia Haworth, upon the condition that she, the said Miss Celia Haworth, shall during my life time take care of and look after me, giving me the best of care and attention. All expenses to be paid by the said Miss Celia Haworth out of my property for the taking care of maintenance of me during my life time.

4.   I hereby appoint my beloved husband, William A. Stephan, to be Executor of this my last Will and Testament, and do hereby direct and request the court to appoint the said William A. Stephan without bond.

In testimony Whereof I have hereunto caused this my last Will and Testament to be signed by John Andrews for me, and I do hereby in the presence of John Andrews and in the presence of F.E. Turner declare this to be my last Will and Testament.

Dated at Chautauqua, Kansas, this the 15th day of June, 1914.

her
Madeline X Stephan
mark

The above and foregoing instrument of writing signed by John Andrews for Madeline Stephan, sealed, published and declared by Madeline Stephan as her last Will and Testament, and we at her request and in her presence and in the presence of each other do hereby sign this Instrument of writing as witnesses thereto.

Dated at Chautauqua, Kansas, this the 15th day of June, 1914.

John Andrews
F.E. Turner.

LETTERS TESTAMENTARY.

The State of Kansas, Chautauqua County, as.

THE STATE OF KANSAS,
To All Persons to Whom These Presents Shall Come---Greeting:

KNOW YE, That the last Will and Testament of **Madeline Stephan** deceased, hath in due form of Law been exhibited, proved and recorded in the office of the Probate Court of Chautauqua County, a copy of which is hereto annexed; and it appearing that **William A. Stephan** is named in said Will as executor thereof. To the end, therefore, that the property may be preserved for those who shall appear to have a legal right or interest in the same, and that the Will may be executed according to the request of the Testator. We do hereby authorize the said **William A. Stephan** as suck executor to collect and secure all and singular, the goods, chattels, rights and credits, which were of the said **Madeline Stephan** at the time of **her** death, in whosoever hands or possession the same may be found, and to perform and fulfill all such duties as may be enjoined upon **him** by said Last Will, so far as there shall be property, and in general to do and perform all other acts which are now or may hereafter be required of **him** by law.

IN TESTIMONY WHEREOF, I **A.M. Ross** Judge of the Probate Court, in and for the County of Chautauqua aforesaid, have hereunto subscribed my name and affixed the Seal of said Court at office, this **8** day of **July** A.D. 1915.

A.M. Ross

Probate Judge.

Department of The Interior,
Office of Indian Affairs, Washington,

JAN 15 1917

It is respectfully recommended that the within will (certified copy) be approved in pursuance of the Act of June 25, 1910 (36 Stats. L., 855-6) as amended by Act of February 14, 1913 (37 Stats. L., 678).

Respectfully,

EB Meritt

Assistant Commissioner.

Department of The Interior
Office of The Secretary JAN 23 1917

The within will (certified copy) is hereby approved in pursuance of the Act of June 25, 1910 (36 Stats. L., 855-6) as amended by Act of February 14, 1913 (37 Stats. L., 678).

Bo Sweeney

Assistant Secretary

▲ ▼ ▲ ▼ ▲ ▼ ▲ ▼ ▲ ▼ ▲ ▼ ▲ ▼ ▲ ▼

PON-CA-SA JEWETT

OFFICE OF INDIAN AFFAIRS
RECEIVED
NOV 2 - 1918
114114

LAST WILL AND TESTAMENT OF PON-CA-SA, JEWETT 114114

In the name of God Amen.

I pon-ca-sa[sic] Jewett being of sound mind and memory do make, publish and declare this to be my last will and testament hereby revokeing[sic] all former wills by me made,

First.- I direct that all of my debts and funeral charges e paid out of the money belonging to me now in the hands of the Superintendent in trust for me at Macy Nebraska,

Second.- I give to my daughter Sarah Thomas Blackbird and to my son Paul Thomas share and share alike The west one half and the north-east quarter of the south-east quarter of section two (2) in township twenty-five (25) north of range nine (9) east of the 6th P.M. in Thurston County Nebr.

Third.- To my daughter Sarah Thomas Blackbird The north-east quarter of the North-east fractional quarter of section three (3) in Township twety[sic] four north of range nine east of the 6th, P.M. in Thurston county, Nebraska together with the improvements thereon,

Fourth To my son Paul Thomas I give and bequeathe the north-west quarter of the north-east quarter of section three (3) in township twenty four (24) north of range nine (9) east of the 6th P.M. in Thurston County Nebr,

Fifth- I give and bequeathe to my said Son and daughter hereinbefore named share and share alike what money there may be left in the hands of the Superintendant[sic] at Macy to my credit after paying my debts and funeral charges as hereinbefore mentioned, also any lands that I mw[sic] be heir to

Lastly I hereby appoint my friend Thomas R. Ashley of Decatur, Nebraska Executor of this my last will and testament,
In witness whereof I have hereunto affixed my name by making the mark by impression of my right thumb, This 28th day of February 1916 her

Pon ca sa-Jewett [thumb print]
mark

We whose names are hereunto subscribed do hereby certify that the above will was signed by the testator in our presence and in the presence of each of us and we do sign our names hereto as subscribeing[sic] witnesses at her request.

Bert Fremont
Chas Thomas
Both of Thurston County, Nebraska

114114-1916

Department of The Interior,
Office of Indian Affairs, Washington,
JAN 24 1917
The within will of Poncasah Jewett Omaha allottee #746-N is herewith recommended for approval in pursuance of the Act of June 25, 1910 (36 Stats. L., 855-6) as amended by Act of February 14, 1913 (37 Stats. L., 678).

Respectfully,
EB Meritt
Assistant Commissioner

Department of The Interior
Office of The Secretary JAN 30 1917

The within will of Poncasah Jewett dated February 28, 1916, is hereby approved in pursuance of the Act of June 25, 1910 (36 Stats. L., 855-6) as amended by Act of February 14, 1913 (37 Stats. L., 678). No executor, however, will be recognized.

Bo Sweeney
Assistant Secretary

▲▼▲▼▲▼▲▼▲▼▲▼▲▼▲▼

FRANCES SUTTON
Will

Siletz, Oregon February 5, 1914

I, Frances Sutton, of lawful age and of sound mind in the presence of witnesses assembled at my request desire to publish this my last will hereby revoking any and all former wills by me made.

All my just debts shall be paid from my estate.

First: I give and bequeath my own allotment described as the S^2 SW^4 Sec 4, T10 S. R 9 W. W.M., 80 acres to my son Newton Sutton.

Second: I give and bequeath all my interest in the allotment of my deceased relative Sarah Captain, the Lots 7, 10, 11, 12 Sec. 4, T 10 S., R 9W. W.M. 82.87 acres and also that of John Captain which I claim through her W^2E^2 & E^2W^2 SE^4 Sec 4, T 10 S. R 9W. W.M., 80 acres; the former to Anna Smith and the latter to my son Newton Sutton.

Third: I claim to have inherited the allotment of John Skelly described as Lots 25, 26, 27 & 28 Sec 11 & Lots 1, 2 & 3 Sec. 14-7-11= 80 acres and that of his wife Catherine Skelly described as Lots 9, 10 & 11 Sec. 11 & Lot 16 Sec 10, T 7 S, R 11 W. W.M., Oregon, 80 acres. I wish my son Newton Sutton to have all my interest in the aforesaid allotment of John Skelly and I wish my niece Anna Smith to have all my interest in the aforesaid allotment of Catherine Skelly.

Provided that when any of the inherited allotments mentioned are sold my nephew Joseph Steve shall have one hundred dollars of the proceeds of each thereof.

Witnesses:	her
John Adams	*Frances Sutton* [thumb print]
W.F. Prince	mark

Acknowledged subscribed & sealed before us this 5th day of February, 1914.

Knott Egbert

Department of The Interior,
Office of Indian Affairs, Washington,

JAN 27 1917

The will of Frances Sutton dated February 5, 1915, is hereby recommended for approval, in accordance with the Act of June 25, 1910 (36 Stats. L., 855-6) as amended by Act of February 14, 1913 (37 Stats. L., 678), but no right of an Executor or Executrix is recognized therein.

Respectfully,
EB Meritt
Assistant Commissioner.

Department of The Interior
Office of The Secretary FEB -1 1917

The will of Frances Sutton dated February 5, 1914, is hereby approved in accordance with the Act of June 25, 1910 (36 Stats. L., 855-6) as amended by Act of February 14, 1913 (37 Stats. L., 678), but no right of an Executor or Executrix is recognized therein.

Bo Sweeney
Assistant Secretary

▲ ▼ ▲ ▼ ▲ ▼ ▲ ▼ ▲ ▼ ▲ ▼ ▲ ▼

WILLIAM CRAZY BULL (WILLIAM JONES)

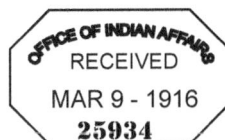

WILL.

OFFICE OF INDIAN AFFAIRS
RECEIVED
MAR 9 - 1916
25934

In the name of God, Amen:

I, William Crazy Bull, (William Jones), of the county of Tripp, and the state of South Dakota, being of full age, and sound mind, do make, publish and declare this my last will and testament, that is to say.

First. I direct that all my lawful debts, the expenses of my last sickness and burial, and of the administration of my estate, be first paid, and subject thereto:-

Second. I give devise and bequeath to my beloved wife, Julia Walker Crazy Bull, the following personal property, to-wit: One gray mare, eight years old; one bay gilding, eight years old; one bay gilding, two years old; one buckskin yearling horse colt; one log house; two lumber wagons; one saddle; one mower machine; one hay rake and hay sweep, and one hay rack. I also give and bequeath to my wife, names herein, an undivided one half interest in and to 320 acres of land owned by me in Tripp County, this state, which said land is a government allotment, and I hereby request that the said one half interest in and to the said allotment mentioned herein, be and it is given to my said wife.

Third. I give, devise and bequeath to my mother, Emma Crazy Bull, and my sister, Mary Crazy Bull, in equal shares the following personal property, to-wit: One bay mare, eight years old; one bay gilding seven years old; one bay gilding, eight years old; one two seated spring wagon, and harness whcih[sic] is used with the said wagon. I also give and bequeath to my mother and sister named above, in equal shares, the remaining undivided one half interest in and to my allotment located in Tripp County, this state, and it is my desire that the said land as devised and (*the rest of the paragraph illegible*).

Fourth. And lastly, I give, devise and bequeath all of the rest and residue of my said property of which I die seized to my wife, Julia Walker Crazy Bull, of ever[sic] kind and character. And I hereby nominate *A. N. Coe* my executor of this my last will and testament.

I further desire to state, that my mother was the plural wife of my father, Crazy Bull, but that for the last *two* years, he has abandoned her, and has never contributed in any way to her support, or to that of my sister, Mary Crazy Bull, and it is my earnest desire that no part of my said property be given to him, and for this reason I have made no provision that he should have any part of my estate, and that my government allotment should be disposed of in the manner designated in the foregoing will.

In witness whereof I have hereto subscribed my name at Bill Creek, in the county of Tripp, and the state of South Dakota, this 24th day of May, 1915.

William Crazy Bull
William Jones

The foregoing written instrument consisting of two sheets of paper, was on the 24th day of May, 1915, subscribed b the testator, William Crazy Bull, as and for his last will and testiment[sic] in the presence of Isaac Battelyoun, and Sussan[sic] Battelyoun, the undersigns herein, in the presence of each of them, who at his request and in the presence of each other, have signed our names hereto as subscribing witnesses.

Isaac Battelyoun
Susan Battelyoun

Department of The Interior,
Office of Indian Affairs, Washington,

JAN 24 1917

The within will is hereby recommended for approval in pursuance of the Act of June 25, 1910 (36 Stats. L., 855-6) as amended by the Act of

February 14, 1913 (37 Stats. L., 678), but no right of an executor or executrix is recognized in connection therewith.

> Respectfully,
> *EB Meritt*
> Assistant Commissioner

Department of The Interior
Office of The Secretary   JAN 29 1917

The within will is hereby recommended for approval in pursuance of the Act of June 25, 1910 (36 Stats. L., 855-6) as amended by the Act of February 14, 1913 (37 Stats. L., 678), but no right of an executor or executrix is recognized in connection therewith.

> *Bo Sweeney*
> Assistant Secretary

▲▼▲▼▲▼▲▼▲▼▲▼▲▼

MA-NA-KU-GAE or WILLIAM FROST

6165-1916
Omaha Agency

IN THE NAME OF GOD, AMEN.

****

I, Ma-na-ku-gae or William Frost, of the Omaha Reservation in the County of Thurston, State of Nebraska, being of sound mind and memory, and considering the uncertainties of this frail and transitory life, do therefore, make, ordain, publish and declare this to be my LAST WILL AND TESTAMENT:

FIRST. I order and direct that my EXECUTOR hereinafter named, pay all my just debts and funeral expenses as soon after my decease as conveniently may be.

SECOND. After the payment of such funeral expenses and debts, I give, devise and bequeath unto my grand daughter, Fannie Frost Woodhall, eighty (80) acres of land, being the East Half (E.1/2) of the land allotted to me as a member of the Omaha Tribe of Indians, and for which I now hold a trust patent, and being described as follows, viz: the South East Quarter of Sewction Twenty-five (SE1/4 of Sec. 25) in Township Twenty-four (Twp. 24) North of Range Nine (9) East of the

6th P.M. in the State of Nebraska, containing One Hundred Sixty (160) acres. The legal description of the land which I hereby give, devise and bequeath unto my grand daughter, Fannie Frost Woodhall, being the East One-half (E.1/2) of the South East Quarter (SE1/4) of Section Twenty-five (Sec. 25) in Township Twenty-four (Twp. 24) North of Range Nine (9) East of the 6th P.M. in the State of Nebraska, containing Eighty (80) acres.

THIRD. I also give, devise and bequeath unto my grand daughter, Rose Dick Porter, the South West Quarter (SW1/4) of the South East Quarter (SE1/4) Section Twenty-five (Sec. 25) in Township Twenty-four (Twp. 24) North of Range Nine (9) East of the 6th P.M. in the State of Nebraska, containing Forty (40) acres.

Fourth[sic]. I also give, devise and bequeath unto my grand sons, George Dick and Mitchell Dick, the North West Quarter (NW1/4) of the South East Quarter (SE1/4) of the Section Twenty-five (Sec. 25) in Township Twenty-four (Twp. 24) North of Range Nine (9) East of the 6th P.M. in the State of Nebraska, containing Forty (40) acres, each to have an equal undivided interest in the said forty acres hereby bequeath to them.

FIFTH. All the residue and remainder of my estate both real and personal of which I may be seized at the time of my death, I hereby give, devise and bequeath unto my aforesaid grand daughter, Fannie Frost Woodhall.

LASTLY. I make constitute and appoint my friend Guy Stab to be EXECUTOR of this my last will and testament, hereby revoking all former wills by me made.

IN WITNESS WHEREOF I have hereunto subscribed my name and affixed my seal this 21st day of January, in the year of our Lord, One Thousand, Nine Hundred and Fourteen.

his
William Frost [thumb print]
mark

This instrument was on the day of the date thereof signed published and declared by the said testator, Ma-na-ku-gae or William Frost, to be his last will and testament, in the presence of us, who at his request have subscribed our names thereto and in the presence of each other as witnesses, and we are each witnesses to the thumb mark of the said testator made by him on this will in our presence.

WITNESSES: *Grover Haclaw*   *Thomas Reese*
                                Hair Reese   *PH Konziom*

6165-16
Omaha.

Department of The Interior,
Office of Indian Affairs, Washington,
NOV -4 1916

The within will of William Frost, is hereby recommended for approval in pursuance of the Act of June 25, 1910 (36 Stats. L., 855-6) as amended by the Act of February 14, 1913 (37 Stats. L., 678), but no right of an executor or executrix is recognized in connection therewith.

                       Respectfully,
                       EB Meritt
                       Assistant Commissioner

Department of The Interior
Office of The Secretary   NOV 15 1916

The within will of William Frost, is hereby recommended for approval in pursuance of the Act of June 25, 1910 (36 Stats. L., 855-6) as amended by the Act of February 14, 1913 (37 Stats. L., 678), but no right of an executor or executrix is recognized in connection therewith.

                       Bo Sweeney
                       Assistant Secretary

FLYING WOMAN
"WILL"

OFFICE OF INDIAN AFFAIRS
RECEIVED
NOV 20 1916
119752

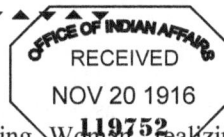

IN THE NAME OF GOD AMEN; I Flying Woman, realizing the uncertainties of this life; and while I am still of sound mind and disposing memory, do make publish and declare this my last Will and Testament; hereby revoking all former wills or codicils made by myself.

Indian Wills, 1911 – 1921 Book Three
Records of The Bureau of Indian Affairs

It is my will that after my death, all of my just debts and funeral expenses be paid; and the remainder of my property I despose[sic] of as follows;-

To my son Thomas, W1/2 of SE1/4 of Sec. 14 Twp 15 Range 12 W.I.M.

To my son Rollin, NE1/4 of SE1/4 of Sec. 14 Twp. 15 Range 12 W.I.M.

To my Husband, Blowaway, SE1/4 of SE1/4 Sec. 14 Twp. 15 Range 12 W.I.M.

All land I may have inherited to be disposed of in accordance with the law of the state.

All of my personal property not mentioned above to my Husband Blowaway.

This will to be submitted to the Secretary of the Interior through the Supt. of the Cheyenne & Arapaho Agency at Concho, Okla.

In witness whereof I have signed, sealed, published and declared this instrument consisting of two typewritten sheets to be my last Will and Testament at Watonga, Oklahoma, this 11th day of June, 1916.

her
FLYING WOMAN   [thumb print]
mark

That said Flying Woman at Watonga Oklahoma, on the 11th day of June 1916, signed and sealed this instrument, and published and declared the same as and for her last will and testament, and we at her request and in her presence and in the presence of each other, have here onto written our names as subscribing witnesses.

AV Crotzer - Farmer
M.B. Crotzer - Notary Public

Law-Heirship
132530-16
S E B

Department of The Interior,
Office of Indian Affairs, Washington,
> FEB -2 1917

The within will of Flying Woman, is recommended for approval in accordance with the Act of June 25, 1910 (36 Stats. L., 855-6) as amended by the Act of February 14, 1913 (37 Stats. L., 678).

Respectfully,
EB Meritt
Assistant Commissioner

Department of The Interior
Office of The Secretary
> FEB 10 1917

The within will of Flying Woman, is recommended for approval in accordance with the Act of June 25, 1910 (36 Stats. L., 855-6) as amended by the Act of February 14, 1913 (37 Stats. L., 678).

Bo Sweeney
Assistant Secretary

▲▼▲▼▲▼▲▼▲▼▲▼▲

OFFICE OF INDIAN AFFAIRS
RECEIVED
JAN 8- 1917
2381

CHARLIE KEBOLTE

NO. 1804

Filed Mar. 21 - 1016.
Jas.A.Embry, Court Clerk

I, Charlie Kebolte of Tohee Twonship[sic], Lincoln County, Okla. being of sound mind and memory do make publish and declare this to be my last Will and Testament to-wit:

First: All my just debts and funeral expenses shall be first be[sic] duly paid.

Second: I give devise and bequeath all the rest, residue and remainder all of my Real estate estate[sic] both personal to my House Servant Mrs. Florinda Cramer to have and hold to her my said House Servant and to her heirs and assignes[sic] for ever.

Third: I nominate and appoint C.N. Christ to be the executor of this my last will and testament, hereby revoke[sic] all former will[sic] by me made.

In Witness Whereof I have hereunto set my hand and seal this 27th of February 1916 A.D.

Signed sealed published and declared as and for his last will Testament by the above named Testator in our presence who have at his request and his presence and in the presence of each other, signed our names as witness thereto[sic].

Chas. Kebolte.

Witnesses
C.N. Christ,
Aaron W. Christ
Josiphina[sic] Miller.

Department of The Interior,
Office of Indian Affairs, Washington,
JAN 17 1917

The within instrument dated February 27, 1916, and certified by the Court Clerk of Lincoln County, Oklahoma to be a true, correct and complete copy of the will of Charles Kebolts, deceased, is hereby recommended for approval pursuant to the Act of June 25, 1910 (36 Stats. L., 855-6) as amended by the Act of February 14, 1913 (37 Stats. L., 678), so far as it relates to the interest of the testator in land included in the allotment of Eliza White Kebolte, deceased Iowa allottee No. 54.

Respectfully,
EB Meritt
Assistant Commissioner

Department of The Interior
Office of The Secretary *Feb 21 1917*

The within instrument certified to be a true, correct and complete copy of the will of Charles Kebolte, deceased, is hereby approved so far as it relates to the testator's interest in the allotment of Eliza White Kebolte, deceased Iowa allottee No. 54, in pursuance of the Act of June 25, 1910 (36 Stats. L., 855-6) as amended by the Act of February 14, 1913 (37 Stats. L., 678), nothing in this approval contained to be construed as recognizing any authority or jurisdiction on the part of the executor of said will over the land included in said allotment.

Bo Sweeney
Assistant Secretary

▲▼▲▼▲▼▲▼▲▼▲▼▲▼▲▼

JOHN HARRISON

Indian Wills, 1911 – 1921 Book Three
Records of The Bureau of Indian Affairs

LAST WILL AND TESTAMENT OF

JOHN HARRISON

I, John Harrison, being of sound mind and disposing memory, and of good health, but realizing the uncertainties of life do hereby make, publish, and declare this to be my LAST WILL AND TESTAMENT as follows:

1st, To my son, William Harrison, I give, devise, and bequeath that portion of my allotment upon the Winnebago Reservation in Nebraska described as the Northeast quarter of the Northeast quarter of section ten (10), township twenty-six (26) North of range six (6) east of the Sixth Principal Meridian and containing forty acres according to the U.S. Government survey.

2nd, To my daughter, Helen Harrison Rave, I give, devise, and bequeath that portion of my allotment described the southwest quarter of the northeast quarter of section ten (10), township twenty-six (26) North of range six (6) east of the Sixth Principal Meridian and containing forty acres according to the U.S. Government survey.

3rd, to my son, Charles Harrison, I give, devise, and bequeath that portion of my allotment described as the Southeast quarter of the Northeast quarter of section ten (10), township twenty-six (26) North of range six (6) east of the Sixth Principal Meridian and containing forty acres according to the U.S. Government survey.

John Harrison

The said testator at this time signed his name to the above and foregoing instrument in the presence of the undersigned and at the same time declared it to be his LAST WILL AND TESTAMENT, and we at his request, and in his presence, and in the presence of each other do hereby sign our names witnesses.

Sam Young
Hugh Hantin

Winnebago Agency, Nebraska,
 April 10, 1915.

63919-1916

37

Indian Wills, 1911 – 1921 Book Three
Records of The Bureau of Indian Affairs

Department of The Interior,
Office of Indian Affairs, Washington,
FEB 17 1917
It is recommended that the attached will of John Harrison, deceased
Winnebago allottee No. 225, be approved in pursuance of the provisions
of the Act of June 25, 1910 (36 Stats. L., 855-6) as amended by Act of
February 14, 1913 (37 Stats. L., 678).

> Respectfully,
> *EB Meritt*
> Assistant Commissioner

Department of The Interior
Office of The Secretary

The within will of John Harrison, deceased Winnebago No. 225 is hereby
approved by authority of the Act of June 25, 1910 (36 Stats. L., 855-6) as
amended by Act of February 14, 1913 (37 Stats. L., 678).

> *Bo Sweeney*
> Assistant Secretary

▲▼▲▼▲▼▲▼▲▼▲▼▲▼▲▼

THOMAS CADOTTE

IN THE NAME OF GOD, AMEN.

I, Thomas Cadotte of the County of Barage, State of Michigan,
being of sound and disposing mind and memory, and considering the
uncertainty of this life, do make, publish and declare this to be my last
Will and Testament as follows:

First; after my lawful debts are paid, I give, devise and bequeath
to my sister Lucy Cadotte, the following described land to wit: South
West quarter of South West Quarter Section Twenty-five (25) Township
Fifty (50) North of Range Thirty-three (33) West, containing Fourty[sic]
(40) acres, also one book called The Complete Compendium of Universal
Knowledge, and my ring: to have and to hold the same to the said Lucy
Cadotte her heirs and assigns to her and their use and behoof[sic] forever.

Second: I give, devise and bequeath to my sister Maggie Cadotte
the following described land to wit: South East Quarter of South West

Quarter Section Twenty-five (25) Township Fifty (50) North of Range Thirty-three (33) West, containing Fourty[sic] (40) acres, also my trunk. To have and to hold the same to the said Maggie Cadotte her heirs and assigns to her and their use and behoof[sic] forever.

And last: I hereby appoint my said sister Lucy Cadotte to be executor of this my last will and testament, revoking and annulling all former Wills by me made, and ratifying and confinning[sic] this nad[sic] no other, to be my Last Will and Testament.

In witness Whereof, I have hereunto set my hand and seal this fourth day of May, in the year of our Lord one thousand nine hundred and three.

THOMAS CADOTTE, (SEAL)

Signed, declared and published by the above-named Thomas Cadotte, as and for his last Will and Testament, in presence of us, who, at his request, and in his presence, and in the presence of each other, have signed as witnesses to the same this fourth day of May, in the year of our Lord one thousand nine hundred and three.

Edward Cadotte, of Assinins
Mrs. Mary Jane Enerie of L'Anse.

State of Michigan,
The Probate Court for the County of *Baraga*
In the Matter of the Estate of *Thomas Cadotte*

Deceased

I *John H McLean Judge* of said court, having the legal custody of the files and records thereof do hereby certify that I have compared the attached copy of
will of said deceased
certificate on Probate of will
Proof on Probate of will

With the original thereof on file in said court and have found the same to be a correct transcript therefrom, and of the whole of such original*s*---

In Testimony Whereof, I have hereunto set

my hand and affixed the seal of said court, at the *Village of Lanse* in said county this *28th* day of *December* A.D. 19*14*

John H McLean
Judge of Probate

Law-Heirship
107652-16
127130-16
CET

Department of The Interior,
Office of Indian Affairs, Washington, D.C.

FEB 15 1917   1917.

I have the honor to recommend that the certified copy of the will of Thomas Cadotte, deceased Chippewa allottee No. 165, be laid before the President for his approval, under the provisions of the Treaty of September 30, 1854 (10 Stats. L. 1109).

Cate Sells
Commissioner

Department of The Interior
Office of The Secretary

I have the honor to recommend that the certified copy of the will of Thomas Cadotte, deceased Chippewa allottee No. 165, be approved under the provisions of the Treaty of September 30, 1854 (10 Stats. L. 1109).

Franklin K Payne
Secretary

The White House,
    20 February   1917
    Approved:
        Woodrow Wilson
        STATE OF MICHIGAN

THE PROBATE COURT FOR THE COUNTY OF BARAGA.

At a session of said court, held at the Probate Office in the Village of L'Anse, in said County, on the 2nd day of December, A. D. 1907

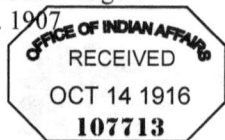

OFFICE OF INDIAN AFFAIRS
RECEIVED
OCT 14 1916
107713

Indian Wills, 1911 – 1921 Book Three
Records of The Bureau of Indian Affairs

PRESENT, HON. JAMES McMAHAN, Judge of Probate.

IN THE MATTER OF THE ESTATE OF THOMAS CADOTTE,
Deceased.

Adjourned Hearing on petition of Lucy Cadotte, for the probate of an instrument in writing purporting to be the last will and testament of said deceased.

Evidence of _____ of notice of hearing filed.

Petitioner appeared in person and by J. J. O'Connor, her attorney.

Edward Cadotte being duly sworn and examined as a witness on behalf of the petitioner, to prove the last will and testament of said deceased, testified as follows:

I reside in the Township of Baraga, in the county of Baraga, and state of Michigan. I was acquainted with said deceased, in his life time. At the time of his death, he was a resident of the Township of L'Anse, in said county, and died on or about the 29th day of May, 1903.

I am one of the subscribing witnesses to the instrument now on file in said court, and now shown to me, purporting to the the[sic] last will and tetament of said deceased. On the 4th day of May, 1903, at the Township of L'Anse, in the county of Baraga and state of Michigan, said deceased signed and sealed said instrument in the presence of myself and Mrs. Mary Hane Emerie, late of the Twp. of L'Anse, County of Baraga, Mich, the other subscribing witness thereto. The said deceased, then and there, in our presence, published and declared the said instrument to be his last will and testament, and then and there requested us to subscribe our names to said instruments as witnesses thereto. We did thereupon, then and there, at the request of said deceased, in his presence, and in the presence of each other, subscribe our names to said instrument as witnesses thereto.

The said deceased, at the time his signed, sealed, published and declared the said instrument as aforesaid, was above the age of twenty-one years, and according to my discernment and belief, of sound mind, and under no restraint or undue influence whatever.

Subscribed and sworn to before me, this 2nd, day of December, A. D. 1907.

JAMES McMAHAN
Judge of Probate.

STATE OF MICHIGAN

THE PROBÁTE COURT FOR THE COUNTY OF BARAGA.

IN THE MATTER OF THE ESTATE OF THOMAS CADOTTE,
Deceased.

I, James McMahan, judge of said court, do hereby certify that the annexed instrument was this day duly proved and allowed as the last will and testament of Thomas Cadotte, late of the Township of Baraga, in said county, deceased.

IN TESTIMONY WHEREOF, I have hereunto set my hand and affixed the seal of said court, at the Village of L'Anse, in said county, this 2nd, day of December, A. D. 1907.

(SEAL)　　　　　　　　James McMahan,
Judge of Probate.

▲▼▲▼▲▼▲▼▲▼▲▼▲▼
MAGGIE LAMOREAUX

WILL.

I, Maggie Lamoreaux, of the City of Bayfield in the County of Bayfield, in the State of Wisconsin, being of sound mind and memory do make, publish and declare this my last will and testament, hereby revoking all former wills, bequests and devises by me made.

1st. It is my will that all of my just debts, funeral expenses and charges be paid out of any property that I may own at the time of my death, or to which I may be entitled.

2nd. I give and bequeath to the Holy Family Catholic Congregation of Bayfield, Wisconsin, the sum of Two Hundred Dollars

42

($200.00) and I request that the pastor and authorities of said Church hold appropriate services and say masses for the repose of my soul as may be appropriate and in accord with the usages and practices of said Church.

3rd. All the rest and residue of my estate, real, personal or mixed whether in possession or otherwise, I hereby give, devise and bequeath to my nephews and nieces as follows: Maggie Gordon, Maggie Neveaux, Joseph Neveaux, Mary Bresette, Joseph Lamoreaux, Francis Lamoreaux, Eli Lamoreaux, John Lamoreaux and Albert Lamoreaux to each an equal, undivided share of said residue, the said nephews and nieces to take such residue exclusively, and free from all claims of any relatives or persons who might claim said estate had I died intestate.

4th. I do make, constitute and appoint A. J. Wilkinson as executor of this my last will and testament, giving him power and authority to sell and convey any property, real or personal of which I may die seized, such sale and conveyance to be made for the purpose of carrying out the terms of this will.

IN WITNESS WHEREOF I have hereunto set my hand and seal this 31st day of March, A. D. 1915.

Maggie Lamoreaux (Seal)

Signed, sealed, published and declared by the said Maggie Lamereaux as and for her last will and testament, in the presence of us, who at her request, in her presence and in the presence of each other, have hereunto subscribed our names as attesting witnesses.

Mary Bresett Reil   Bayfield, Wisconsin.
John J. Fisher   Bayfield, Wisconsin.

Department of The Interior,
Office of Indian Affairs, Washington,
                FEB 16 1917
The within certified copy of the will of Maggie Lamoreaux, deceased, is hereby recommended for approval in accordance with the provisions of the Act of June 25, 1910 (36 Stats. L., 855, 856) as amended by Act of February 14, 1913 (37 Stats. L., 678, 679), insofar as it applies to personal property under the supervision of the Department

Respectfully,

EB Meritt

Assistant Commissioner

Department of The Interior

Office of The Secretary MAR -1 1917

The within certified copy of the will of Maggie Lamoreaux, deceased, is hereby recommended for approval in accordance with the provisions of the Act of June 25, 1910 (36 Stats. L., 855, 856) as amended by Act of February 14, 1913 (37 Stats. L., 678, 679), insofar as it applies to personal property under the supervision of the Department

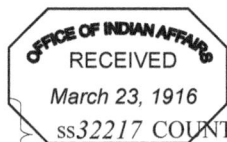

Bo Sweeney

Assistant Secretary

STATE OF WISCONSIN,

OFFICE OF INDIAN AFFAIRS
RECEIVED
March 23, 1916
ss*32217* COUNTY COURT FOR SAID COUNTY

COUNTY OF BAYFIELD

I, **H. P. Axelberg,** County Judge of said County Do Hereby Certify that the Copy hereunto annexed has been compared by me with the Original **Will, petition for Probate of Will, Order Appointing time to Prove Will and fixing time for Claims and Notice to Creditors, Proof of Will not contested, Decree allowing will, and certificate of Proof of Will, in the matter of the Will of Maggie Lamoreaux, deceased,** now on file and of record in my office, and required by law to be in my custody; and that said coy is a true copy thereof.

In testimony whereof I have hereunto set my hand and affixed the seal of the County Court of Bayfield County, at the City of Washburn, in said County this **15th** day of **March** A.D. 191**6**.

H. P. Alexberg

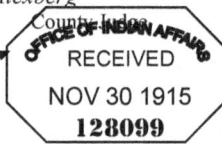

OFFICE OF INDIAN AFFAIRS
RECEIVED
NOV 30 1915
128099

MARY REAL RIDER

Last will and Testament.

I, Mary Real Rider, of Pawnee, Pawnee County, Oklahoma a member of the Pawnee Indian Tribe, being now of sound and disposing mind and sensible of the uncertainty of life and desiring to make disposition of my property and affairs while of sound and disposing mind, do hereby make, publish and declare the following to be my last will and testament, hereby revoking and cancelling any former will by me at any time made.

First I direct the payment of all my just debts and funeral expenses.

I make this my last will and testament with the full knowledge that I have no children living.

I give and bequeath all my personal property including all moneys to my credit in the office of the Superintendent of the Pawnee Indian Agency after the payment of all my just debts and funeral expenses to my mother, Alice Real Rider and my brother of the full-blood, William Real Rider in equal shares.

I give and devise to my brother of the full-blood, William Real Rider to the exclusion of my brother of the half-blood, Warren Real Rider and to the exclusion of my mother, Alice Real Rider because of the fact that the said William Real Rider is not an allottee of the Pawnee tribe whereas the said Alice Real Rider and Warren Real Rider are allottees of said tribe, my two-ninths (2/9) interest in and to the following described real estate; the allotment of Robert Real Rider, deceased described as the Southwest quarter (1/4) of Section Fourteen (14), Township 21 North, Range Four (4) East and the allotment of Charles Real Rider, described as the Northwest quarter (1/4) of Section Twenty-three (23) Township Twenty-one (21) North Range four (4) East.

I hereby appoint and designate James H. Hale of Pawnee, Oklahoma sole executor, with bond, of this my last will and testament.

In witness whereof, I, Mary Real Rider have to this my last will and testament subscribed my name this 24th day of November, 1915.

Mary Real Rider

Subscribed by Mary Real Rider, in the presence of us the undersigned and at the same time declared by her to us to be her last will and testament and we thereupon at the request of Mary Real Rider, in her presence and in the presence of each other sign our names hereto as witnesses this 24th day of November, 1915, at Pawnee, Oklahoma.

R. E. Waggoner
Rayh P Stanton

State of Oklahoma   )
) ss.
County of Pawnee   )

     I, Mary Real Rider, hereby affirm that I have excluded Warren Real Rider, my brother of the half-blood from participation in the provisions of the above will by reason of the fact that he is a regularly enrolled allottee of the Pawnee tribe and a young able-bodied man of such abilities that he should be able to amply provide for himself and family

Mary Real Rider

Subscribed to and sworn to before me this 24th day of November, 1915.

Frank Hudson
Notary Public

128099-1915
  S E B

Department of The Interior,
Office of Indian Affairs, Washington,
               FEB 12 1917
The within will of Mary Real Rider, is recommended for approval in accordance with the Act of June 25, 1910 (36 Stats. L., 855-6) as amended by the Act of February 14, 1913 (37 Stats. L., 678).

Respectfully,
EB Meritt
Assistant Commissioner

Department of The Interior
Office of The Secretary FEB 26 1917
The within will of Mary Real Rider, is recommended for approval in accordance with the Act of June 25, 1910 (36 Stats. L., 855-6) as amended by the Act of February 14, 1913 (37 Stats. L., 678).

Bo Sweeney
Assistant Secretary

OFFICE OF INDIAN AFFAIRS
RECEIVED
OCT 17 1916
108727

▲▼▲▼▲▼▲▼▲▼▲▼▲▼▲
MARY A BALDWIN

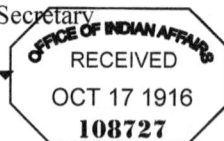

Indian Wills, 1911 – 1921 Book Three
Records of The Bureau of Indian Affairs

Shawnee, Okla. Oct. 6, 1916
At home of Mrs. J. H. Moore
near Dale, Okla.

To Whom It May Concern:

Being in my right mind and without persuasion and after much thought and consideration I have to here freely state that I wish to cancel my will made and signed Dec. 7, 1915 and approved in the Office of the Secretary of the Interior under date of July 21, 1916, and it is now my desire that no will be made or recognized, but that my estate at my death shall descend to all my heirs in harmony with the law given iny[sic] *such matters. This is all my wish and is true and I freely sign my name here.*

Mary A Baldwin

Signed and witnessed in the presence of, and read and acknowledged before us this 6th day of Oct, 1916, near Dale, Okla.

O.J. Green   Supt
Emaline D Green
Patrick J Shipwash
All of Shawnee, Okla.

Department of The Interior,
Office of Indian Affairs, Washington,
FEB -2 1917
It is recommended that the within revocation of the will of Mary a. Baldwin, approved July 21, 1916, be approved.

Respectfully,
EB Meritt
Assistant Commissioner

Department of The Interior
Office of The Secretary
FEB 20 1917
The within revocation of the will of Mary A. Baldwin, approved July 21, 1916, is hereby approved.

Bo Sweeney
Assistant Secretary

▲▼▲▼▲▼▲▼▲▼▲▼▲▼▲▼

WHITE BEAR

Original *"Exhibit A"*
WILL

─────────

I, **White Bear** of Pine Ridge Agency, South Dakota, number .... do hereby make and declare this to be my last will and testament, in accordance with Section 2 of the Act of June 25, 1910, (36 stat. 855-858) and Act of February 14, 1913, (Public No. 381), hereby revoking all former wills made by me:

1. I hereby direct that as soon as possible after my decease, that all my debts, funeral and testamentary expenses be paid out of my personal estate.

2. I give and devise my allotment on the Pine Ridge Reservation, South Dakota, described as follows:

All of Sec. 35, T. 37 N., R. 46 W, containing 640 acres.

in the following manner:

To my grandson Peter		**I bequeath the SW/4**			**160**
" " "	**John**	"	"	" **SE/4**	**160**
" **"Son "**	**Samuel White Bear**	"	"	" **NE/4**	**160**
" **Wife** "	**Day White Bear**	"	"	" **NW/4**	**160**

3. I give and bequeath all of my personal property of whatsoever nature and wheresoever situated unto

To be divided evenly among the above heirs.

4. All the rest of my property, real or personal, now possessed or hereafter acquired, of whatsoever nature and wheresoever situated, I hereby give, devise and bequeath unto

The house I bequeath to my son Samuel White Bear.

In witness whereof I have hereunto set my hand this **12th** day of **March** 191**5**.

his
White Bear [thumb print]
mark

Witness to signatures by mark
Leonard L Smith
Farmer, Oglala, S.D.

Indian Wills, 1911 – 1921 Book Three
Records of The Bureau of Indian Affairs

Solomon Sutle Killer
Ass't Farmer, Oglala, S.D.

Department of The Interior,
Office of Indian Affairs, Washington,

The within will is hereby recommended for approval in accordance with the Act of June 25, 1910 (36 Stats. L., 855-6) as amended by Act of February 14, 1913 (37 Stats. L., 678).

Respectfully,
E B Meritt
Acting Assistant Commissioner

Department of The Interior
Office of The Secretary JAN 10 1917

The within will is hereby approved in accordance with the provisions of the Act of June 25, 1910 (36 Stats. L., 855-6) as amended by Act of February 14, 1913 (37 Stats. L., 678).

Bo Sweeney
Assistant Secretary

▲▼▲▼▲▼▲▼▲▼▲▼▲▼

MATILDA TALL ELK

Original
WILL

OFFICE OF INDIAN AFFAIRS
RECEIVED
OCT 7 - 1916
105060

I, **Matilda Tall Elk** of Pine Ridge Agency, South Dakota, Allottee number **6495** do hereby make and declare this to be my last will and testament, in accordance with Section 2 of the Act of June 25, 1910, (36 stat. 855-858) and Act of February 14, 1913, (Public No. 381), hereby revoking all former wills made by me:

1. I hereby direct that as soon as possible after my decease, that all my debts, funeral and testamentary expenses be paid out of my personal estate.

2. I give and devise my allotment on the Pine Ridge Reservation, South Dakota, described as follows:

Indian Wills, 1911 – 1921 Book Three
Records of The Bureau of Indian Affairs

Lot 4 & E/2 of SE/4 of Sec. 2, T 36, R 45; and SE/4 of SW/4 of Sec. 31, T 37, R 44. 165.43 acres.

in the following manner:

All of my allotment to my husband, Harry Tall Elk.

SE/4 of Sec. 9 & SE/4 of Sec. 10, T 39, R 35, to my mother, Red Track.

3. I give and bequeath all of my personal property of whatsoever nature and wheresoever situated unto

my mother, Red Track. Property consists of two geldings, set of harness and light wagon.

4. All the rest of my property, real or personal, now possessed or hereafter acquired, of whatsoever nature and wheresoever situated, I hereby give, devise and bequeath unto

my mother, Red Track.

In witness whereof I have hereunto set my hand this 6th day of May 1916

Matilda Tall Elk

The above statement was, this 6th day of May 1916 signed and published by Matilda Tall Elk as her last will and testament, in the joint presence of the undersigned, the said Matilda Tall Elk then being of sound and vigorous mid and free from any constraint or compulsion; whereupon we, being without any interest in the matter other than friendship, and being well acquainted with her but not members of her family, immediately subscribed our names hereto in the presence of each other and of the said testator, for the purpose of attesting the said will, as requested us to do. And that I, ... at the testa.....'s request have written .... name in ink, and that .... affixed .... thumbmarks. *(Note: "........" are areas left blank on the original.)*

		Post Office Address
(No Name Given)	**Farmer**	**Pine Ridge, S. D.**
(No Name Given	**Asst. Farmer**	**Pine Ridge, S. D.**

Pine Ridge, South Dakota.
Oct -2 1916

50

I hereby certify that I have fully inquired into the mental competency of the Indian signing the above will; the circumstances attending the execution of the will; the influence that may have induced its execution, and the names of those entitled to share in the estate under the law of descent in South Dakota: reasons for the disposition of the property proposed by the will differing from disposition had the property descended by operation of law.

I respectfully forward this will with the recommendation that it be .....approved.

John R Brennan
Supt. & Spl. Disb. Agent.

Department of The Interior,
Office of Indian Affairs, Washington,

The within will is hereby recommended for approval in accordance with the provisions of the Act of June 25, 1910 (36 Stats. L., 855-6) as amended by Act of February 14, 1913 (37 Stats. L., 678).

Respectfully,
E B Meritt
Acting Assistant Commissioner

Department of The Interior
Office of The Secretary JAN 11 1917

The within will is hereby approved in accordance with the Act of June 25, 1910 (36 Stats. L., 855-6) as amended by Act of February 14, 1913 (37 Stats. L., 678).

Bo Sweeney
Assistant Secretary

▲ ▼ ▲ ▼ ▲ ▼ ▲ ▼ ▲ ▼

MRS. ELLEN PAINE SWIFT

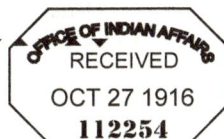

OFFICE OF INDIAN AFFAIRS
RECEIVED
OCT 27 1916
112254

LAST WILL AND TESTAMENT OF ELLEN PAINE,

KLAMATH ALLOTTEE, NO. 396,

Klamath School, Ore.

I, Ellen Paine, now Mrs. Ellen Paine Swift, Klamath Allottee No. 396, aged about 56 years, of the Klamath Reservation, in the County of

Indian Wills, 1911 – 1921 Book Three
Records of The Bureau of Indian Affairs

Klamath And state of Oregon, being of sound mind and memory, do hereby make, publish and declare this, my last will and testament, as follows:-

1st. I direct that my funeral expenses and the expenses of my last illness be paid.

2ndly. I give, devise and bequeath unto William Swift, a white man, aged 48 years, who resides on the Klamath Reservation, County of Klamath and State of Oregon, near the Post Office of Yainax, Oregon, my husband, all my property, both real and personal and mixed, which I may own at the time of my death, or in which I may have any interest, of whatsoever kind the same may be, or wheresoever situated, to have and to hold unto the said William Swift, his heirs and assigns forever.

My real property consists of my allotment on the Klamath Reservation in the County of Klamath, State of Oregon, now held in trust by the United States, and particularly described as follows:- The SW1/4 of the SW 1/4 of Section 10; The South 1/2 of the SE 1/4 of the NE 1/4 and the North 1/2 of the NE 1/4 of the SE 1/4 of Section 16, and the West 1/2 of the NW 1/4 of Section 15, in Township 36 South, of Range 9 East of the Wilamette Meridian, Oregon, containing 160 acres.

3rdly. I hereby revoke any and all former wills by me made.

4thly. I nominate and appoint my husband, William Swife, Executor of this my last will and testament.

In witness hereof, I have hereunto set my hand and seal this 28th day of July, 1916, at Yainax, County of Klamath and State of Oregon.

Ellen Paine Swift
Testatrix.

The foregoing instrument, consisting of One (1) page, was this 28th day of July, 1916, at Yainax, County of Klamath and State of Oregon, by the said Ellen Paine, now Ellen Paine Swift, declared to be her last will and testament and was signed, as such, in our presence, and we, at her request, and in her presence and in the presence of each other, subscribed our names hereunto as subscribing witnesses.

Sargant Brown	Chiloquin, Oregon.
Charles S Minor	Klamath Agency, Oregon.
F.A. Baker	Klamath Agency, Oregon.

112254-16

Department of The Interior,
Office of Indian Affairs, Washington,
JAN 12 1917
The within will, dated July 28th, 1916, of Ellen Paine (now Swift) Klamath Allot. #396, is hereby recommended for approval in accordance with the Act of June 25, 1910 (36 Stats. L., 855-6) as amended by Act of February 14, 1913 (37 Stats. L., 678).

Respectfully,
E B Meritt
Acting Assistant Commissioner

Department of The Interior
Office of The Secretary JAN 12 1917

The within will of Ellen Paine (now Swift), Klamath allottee No. 396, is hereby approved in accordance with the provisions of the Act of June 25, 1910 (36 Stats. L., 855-6) as amended by Act of February 14, 1913 (37 Stats. L., 678). No executor will be recognized in this will.

Bo Sweeney
Assistant Secretary

▲▼▲▼▲▼▲▼▲▼▲▼▲▼

CHO-WY

OFFICE OF INDIAN AFFAIRS
RECEIVED
DEC 4- 1915
129458

DEPARTMENT OF THE INTERIOR

UNITED STATES INDIAN SERVICE

LAST WILL AND TESTAMENT:

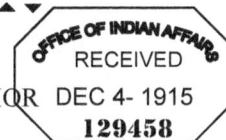

I, Chow y, of ***Faxon, Oklahoma, Comanche*** County, Oklahoma, being now in good health, strength of body and mind, but sensible of the uncertainty of life, and desiring to make disposition of my property and affairs while in health and strength, do hereby make, publish and declare the following to be my last will and testament, hereby revoking and canceling all other or former wills by me at any time made.

First: I direct the payment of all my just debts and funeral expenses.

Second: I give and devise my trust allotment of land, comprising the South West 1/4, Section (22) Township (4) North, Range (11) West of the Indian Meridian in Oklahoma, known as Comanche Indian allotment No. 725, upon the rolls of the Interior Department, to the following persons, and in the shares indicated.

Comanche Indian allottee No. 1665, to Co do-pony, onehalf[sic]; to To wa ka, otherwise known as Cloud Per mam su, Comanche Indian allottee No. 2027, one-fourth; to Pe-pe, Comanche Indian allottee No. 2026, one-fourth.

This will is made subject to the approval of the Secretary of the Interior.

In Witness Whereof, I Cho-wy, Comanche Indian allottee No. 725. have to this my last will and testament, consisting of two sheets of paper, subscribe my name this *13* day of *November*, 1915.

Witness: *Cho-wy*
Anha C Birdsong
Neda Birdsong

Subscribed by Cho wy, Comanche Indian allottee No. 725, in the presence of each of us, the undersigned, and at the same time declared by him to us to be his last will and testament, and we, thereupon, at the request of Chow y, Comanche Indian allottee No. 725, in her[sic] presence, and in the presence of each other, sign our names hereto, as witnesses, this *13* day of *November, 1915*, at *Cache, Okla,* Oklahoma.

Anha C Birdsong
P.O. *Cache, Okla*
Neda Birdsong
P.O. *Cache, Okla.*

INTERPRETER'S CERTIFICATE:

I, *Reuben Tabby to-so-vit*, hereby certify on honor that I acted as interpreter during the execution of the foregoing will of Chow y, Comanche Indian allottee No. 275, and that I truly interpreted all the contents thereof to the testatrix, and that she fully understands all the contents thereof, and that this will was drawn strictly in accordance with her desires and directions. I further certify that I speak both the Comanche and the English languages fluently, and that I have no interest in this matter, whatever.

> *Reuben Tabby Tosovit*
> Interpreter.

129458-15

Department of The Interior,
Office of Indian Affairs, Washington,
                    JAN 10 1917
The within will, dated November 13, 1915, of Cho-wy, Comanche allottee No. 725, is hereby recommended for approval in accordance with the Act of June 25, 1910 (36 Stats. L., 855-6) as amended by Act of February 14, 1913 (37 Stats. L., 678).

> Respectfully,
> *E B Meritt*
> Acting Assistant Commissioner

Department of The Interior
Office of The Secretary   JAN 11 1917

The within will of Cho-wy, Comanche allottee No. 725, is hereby approved in accordance with the provisions of the Act of June 25, 1910 (36 Stats. L., 855-6) as amended by Act of February 14, 1913 (37 Stats. L., 678). No executor will be recognized in this will.

> *Bo Sweeney*
> Assistant Secretary

▲▼▲▼▲▼▲▼▲▼▲▼▲▼

AH-VO-TY

LAST WILL AND TESTAMENT

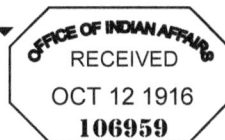

> OFFICE OF INDIAN AFFAIRS
> RECEIVED
> OCT 12 1916
> **106959**

55

Indian Wills, 1911 – 1921 Book Three
Records of The Bureau of Indian Affairs

I, Ah-vo-ty, Kiowa Indian allottee No. 2414, of Mount Scott, Comanche County, Oklahoma, being now in good health, strength of body and mind, but sensible of the uncertainty of life, and desiring to make disposition of my property and affairs while in health and strength, do hereby make, publish and declare the following to be my last will and testament, hereby revoking and cancelling all other and former wills by me at any time made:

1st. I direct the payment of all my just debts and funeral expenses.

2nd. I give and devise to my niece, Julia Given Hunt, Kiowa Indian allottee No. 2813, my trust allotment of land, comprising the Fraction Northeast Quarter of Section Four (4) Township Four (4) North of Range Fourteen (14), West of the Indian Meridian in Okalhoma[sic], known upon the rolls of the Interior Department as Kiowa Indian allotment No. 2414.

3rd. I give and devise to Virginia Sah-maunt, Kiowa Indian allottee No. 2716, all of my interest in and to the Southeast Quarter of Section Four (4) Township Four (4) North of Range Fourteen (14), West of the Indian Meridian in Oklahoma, known upon the rolls of the Interior Department as Kiowa Indian allotment No. 1709. In this allotment I was declared to be an heir in decree of the Department, Law-Heirship 75898-1914, to the extent of one-half thereof.

4th. I give and bequeath all the rest, residue and remainder of my property, real and personal, two-thirds thereof to my said niecre, Julia Given Hunt, Kiowa Allottee No. 2813, and one-third thereof to Virginia Sah-maunt, Kiowa Allottee No. 2716.

This will is made subject to the approval of the Secretary of the Interior.

In witness whereof, I, Ah-vo-ty, have to this my last will and testament, consisting of three sheets of paper, subscribed my name this *31st* day of *July* 1916.

her
Witness: *Ah-vo-ty* [thumb print]
Spencer Witton   m*ark*
H.F. Bretshneider

Subscribed by Ah-vo-ty in the presence of each of us, the undersigned, and at the same time declared by her to us to be her last will and testament, and we thereupon, at the request of Ah-vo-ty, in her presence and in the presence of each other, sign our names hereto as witnesses this *31st* day of *July* 1916, at *Anadarko, Caddo* County, Oklahoma.

> *Spencer Witton*
> *Anadarko, Okla.*(postoffice)
> *H.F. Bretshneider*
> *Anadarko, Okla.*(Postoffice)

OFFICE OF INDIAN AFFAIRS
RECEIVED
OCT 12 1916
106959

INTERPRETER'S CERTIFICATE

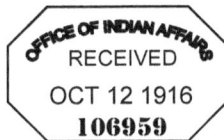

I, *Jasper Saunkeah*, hereby certify on honor that I acted as Interpreter during the execution of the foregoing will by Ah-vo-ty; that she fully understands all the terms and effects thereof, and that the same was drawn strictly in accordance with her desires and directions.

That I speak both the Kiowa Indian and the English languages fluently, and that I have no interest in this matter whatsoever.

Sign this *31* day of *July* 1916.

> *Jasper Saunkeah*
> Interpreter

106959-16

Department of The Interior,
Office of Indian Affairs, Washington,
                    JAN 10 1917
The within will, dated July 31, 1916, of Ah-vo-ty, Kiowa allottee No. 2414, is hereby recommended for approval in pursuance of the Act of June 25, 1910 (36 Stats. L., 855-6) as amended by Act of February 14, 1913 (37 Stats. L., 678).

> Respectfully,
> *E B Meritt*
> Acting Assistant Commissioner

Department of The Interior
Office of The Secretary   JAN 11 1917

Indian Wills, 1911 – 1921 Book Three
Records of The Bureau of Indian Affairs

The within will of Ah-vo-ty, Kiowa allottee No. 2414, is hereby approved in pursuance of the Act of June 25, 1910 (36 Stats. L., 855-6) as amended by Act of February 14, 1913 (37 Stats. L., 678).

Bo Sweeney
Assistant Secretary

▲▼▲▼▲▼▲▼▲▼▲▼▲▼

ONE FEATHER or AH-KU-HI-TU

THE LAST WILL AND TESTAMENT

> OFFICE OF INDIAN AFFAIRS
> RECEIVED
> FEB 27 1911
> **17090**

Of **One Feather or Ah-ku-hi-tu** of the **Fort Berthold Reservation** of **Elbowoods** in the County of **McLean** and State of **North Dakota** made and published the **13th** day of **February** in the year of our Lord one thousand nine hundred and **eleven**.

IN THE NAME OF GOD, AMEN.

I, **One Feather or Ah-ku-hi-tu** of the **Fort Berthold Reservation** of **Elbowoods** in the County of **McLean** and State of **North Dakota** of the age of **seventy eight** years, and being of sound mind and memory, do hereby make, publish and declare this my LAST WILL AND TESTAMENT, in manner following, that is to say:

FIRST - It is my will that my funeral expenses and all my just debts be fully paid.

SECOND - I give and **bequeath to Peter H. Beauchamp my step-grandson the following described allotments, viz:**

The W 1/2 of the NE 1/4 and the W 1/2 of the SE 1/4 Section 24, Township 147 North Range 88, West of the 5th, P.M. containing 160 acres-Allotment No. 750.
I, being the only brother and only legal heir of my own sister Lucky Woman (deceased), convey my Heirship to the following described allotment, to Peter H. Beauchamp. viz:

The E 1/2 of the NE 1/4 Section 13, Township 147 North, Range 88 West of the 5th, P.M. containing 80 acres-Allotment No. 751.

Furthermore; the following described land has been allotted to Tobacco Woman (deceased). The E 1/2 of the SE 1/4, Section 26, Township 148 North, Range 88 West of the 5th P.M. containing 80 acres, and I being her only heir do convey the above described land to my stepson, Yellow Bear.

I also wish that if I live to receive my allotment whatever the description of allotment and number may be under the act of June 1st, 1910, (Public No. 197). I convey the same to said stepson Yellow Bear.

I, One Feather or Ah-ku-hi-tu having no blood relation, consequently no heirs do hereby name the above parties as my heirs.

It is my wish that each party will become heir to my allotments as specified in this my last will, after my decease.

The same said Peter H Beauchamp my step-grandson has contributed to my support since I became old and feeble and will continue to support me until my last day.

LASTLY - I hereby nominate and appoint **John P. Young of Elbowoods, North Dakota** to be the executor of this my Last Will and Testament, hereby revoking all former wills by me made.

IN WITNESS WHEREOF, I have hereunto set my hand and seal the **13th** day of **February** in the year of our Lord one thousand nine hundred and **eleven**.

One Feather   *his*[thumb print] *mark*

The above instrument, consisting of **one** sheet, was now here subscribed by **One Feather or Ah-ku-hi-tu** the Testator in the presence of each of us, and was at the same time declared by **him** to be **his** Last Will and Testament, and we, at **his** request, sign our names hereto in **his** presence as attesting witnesses.

Byron R. Snodgrass   of   *Elbowoods, N. D.*
Anna D. Wilde   of   *Elbowoods, N.D.*

Department of The Interior,
Office of Indian Affairs, Washington, D.C.
MAR 18 1911

Indian Wills, 1911 – 1921 Book Three
Records of The Bureau of Indian Affairs

I hereby recommend that the within will be approved so far as it relates to the original allotment now held in trust for the devisor, namely, the W/2 of the NE/4 and the W/2 of the SE/4, Sec. 24, T. 147 N., R. 88 W. of the 5th P. M., North Dakota, containing 160 acres.

CF Hawke
Approved as recommended: Acting Commissioner.
     Frank (Illegible Last Name)
     First Assistant Secretary

▲▼▲▼▲▼▲▼▲▼▲▼▲▼▲▼

JOSETTE LAUNDRY

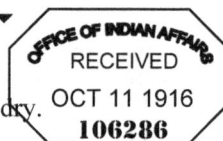

OFFICE OF INDIAN AFFAIRS
RECEIVED
OCT 11 1916
106286

Last Will and Testament of Josette Laundry.

In the name of God, Amen:-

I, Josette Laundry, a member of the Fond du Lac band of Chippewa Indians, age 99 yrs., residing at Cloquet, Minnesota, being of sound mind and memory and realizing the uncertaintities[sic] of life, do hereby make this my last will and testament, revoking all former wills by me made.

-1-

I hereby direct that all my funeral expenses and all my just debts be paid from my estate as soon as may be after my death.

-2-

I give and bequeath to my daughter Lizzie Laundry one house and ten acres of land described as S/4 of NE/4 of SE/4 Sec 9, Twp 49 In of R 17 W of 4th P.M. Minn., together with all the appurtenances and furniture thereto pertaining.

-3-

I give and bequeath to my daughter Lizzie Laundry and to my son Joseph Laundry each an undivided one=half interest in my allotment described as NW/4 of NE/4 & NE/4 of NW/4, Sec 19, T 50, R 17 containg[sic] eighty acres more or less according to Government survey, my daughter Lizzie being 60 yrs. of age and my son Joseph, 58 yrs.

-4-

I give and bequeath one dollar each to my grandchildren Louis E. Laundry and Lizzie Laundry, aged 19 and 16 respectively.

-5-

All other property of which I may die possessed, either real or personal I give, devise and bequeath in equal shares to my daughter Lizzie Laundry and my son Joseph Laundry.

-6-

Reposing full confidence in the integrity of the Supt. of the Fond du Lac reservation, I hereby appoint G.W. Cross, Supt., sole executor of this my last will and testament and it is my desire that he fulfill the duties of said office without being required to file any bond for the faithful performance of his said trust.

In testimony whereof I have hereunto set my hand and seal this 4th day of October, A.D. 1016.

	Her
Witnesses to mark	Josette Laundry [thumb print]
Frank Le Duc	Mark
Joseph Smith	

I, Frank Le Duc, of lawful age, hereby certify that I am acquainted with both the Chippewa and English languages, that I carefully explained the foregoing instrument to Josette Laundry, and that Josette Laundry declared the same to represent her full wishes and desires, and that she was satisfied with the same.

Frank Le Duc
Interpreter.

This instrument, in three pages, was on the date thereof, signed, published and declared by the said testatrix, Josette Laundry, to be her last Will and Testament in our presence, who at her request have subscribed our names thereto as witnesses in her presence and in the presence of each other.

Frank Le Duc Residing at Cloquet, Minn.
Joseph Smith Residing at Cloquet, Minn.

I, Josette Laundry, hereby declare that I am the person who executed the foregoing will and that my reason for devising my property as above is that my daughter Lizzie Laundry has cared for me in my old age and febbleness[sic] for several years and I desire to give her the house and ten acres in recognition of her faithful care and devotion; I do not bequeath anything other than one dollar each to my grandchildren for the reason that they have not contributed to my care and comfort or support.

	Her
Witnesses	Josette Laundry [thumb print]
Frank Le Duc	Mark
Joseph Smith	

Subscribed and sworn to before me this 4th day of October, A.D. 1916, near Cloquet, Minnesota.

> *G. W. Cross*
> Supt. & Spl. D. Agent.

94129-1911
106286-1916

Department of The Interior,
Office of Indian Affairs, Washington,
JAN 10 1917

The within will dated October 4, 1916, of Josette Laundry, Fond du Lac Chippewa allottee No. 4, is hereby recommended for approval in pursuance of the Act of June 25, 1910 (36 Stats. L., 855-6) as amended by the Act of February 14, 1913 (37 Stats. L., 678).

> *EB Meritt*
> Assistant Commissioner

Department of The Interior
Office of The Secretary
JAN 11 1917

The within will of Josette Laundry, Fond du Lac Chippewa allottee No. 4, is hereby approved in pursuance of the Act of June 25, 1910 (36 Stats. L., 855-6) as amended by the Act of February 14, 1913 (37 Stats. L., 678).

> *Bo Sweeney*
> Assistant Secretary

▲ ▼ ▲ ▼ ▲ ▼ ▲ ▼ ▲ ▼ ▲ ▼ ▲ ▼ ▲ ▼

Indian Wills, 1911 – 1921 Book Three
Records of The Bureau of Indian Affairs

BAD HAND or STABBER

OFFICE OF INDIAN AFFAIRS
RECEIVED
SEP 17 1914
100162

OFFICE OF INDIAN AFFAIRS
RECEIVED
MAY 11 1915
53052

WILL Of BAD HAND

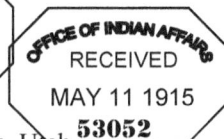

Ft. Duchesne, Utah.
April 2, 1914

KNOW ALL MEN BY THESE PRESENTS, That I, Bad Hand, being of sound mind and memory, do make and declare the following to be my last will and testament; in view of the fact that I have no blood relatives living I feel justified in willing any land that might be allotted to me to Ohiya Bonnin, son of Mr. & Mrs. Raymond T. Bonnin.

I hereby devise and bequeath to Ohiya Bonnin any money which I may have on deposit at the time of my death, and any other property both real and personal that may come to me before my death.

his
Bad Hand [thumb print]
mark

We, Max Bald Eagle, Thomas Crane, Alex Adams, all of Pine Ridge, South Dakota, and Roger C. Mackenstadt, of Ft. Duchesne, Utah, do hereby certify that Bad Hand signed the above will in our presence, and declared at that time that this instrument was his last will and testament; that we sign this will at the request of Bad Hand, in his presence and in the presence of each other.

Witnesses:

Max Bald Eagle	Pine Ridge, S. D.
Interpreter	
Thomas Crane, his [thumb print] mark	" " "
Alex Adams, his [thumb print] mark	" " "
Roger C Mackenstadt	Ft. Duchesne, Utah.

Witnesses to thumb marks signatures

R. T. Bonnin	*Gertrude Bonnin*
Ft. Duchesne, Utah.	Ft. Duchesne, Utah.

33127-12
SEB

Will of Bad Hand
or Stabber

Indian Wills, 1911 – 1921 Book Three
Records of The Bureau of Indian Affairs

Department of The Interior,
Office of Indian Affairs, Washington,
DEC 18 1916

It is recommended that the within will be approved under the Act of June 25, 1910 (36 Stats. L., 855-6) as amended by Act of February 14, 1913 (37 Stats. L., 678).

> Respectfully,
> *E B Meritt*
> Acting Assistant Commissioner

Department of The Interior
Office of The Secretary
DEC 21 1916

The within will is hereby approved under the Act of June 25, 1910 (36 Stats. L., 855-6) as amended by Act of February 14, 1913 (37 Stats. L., 678).

> *Bo Sweeney*
> Assistant Secretary

▲ ▼ ▲ ▼ ▲ ▼ ▲ ▼ ▲ ▼ ▲ ▼ ▲ ▼ ▲ ▼

SAM BINDAY

Law-Heirship
32037-14   DEPARTMENT OF THE INTERIOR
117331-15
  F E   UNITED STATES INDIAN SERVICE

                                          JAN -8 1916
Approval of Verbal   WASHINGTON
Will Mescalero Agency,
New Mexico.

The Honorable,

                  The Secretary of the Interior.
Sir:

I have the honor to transmit herewith the papers in the matter of the will and Heirship case of Sam Binday, an unallotted Apache Indian, who was one of the Apache prisoners of war transferred from Fort Sill, Oklahoma, to the Mescalero Agency, New Mexico.

Indian Wills, 1911 – 1921 Book Three
Records of The Bureau of Indian Affairs

It appears from the evidence in the case and the report of the superintendent that Sam Binday died May 8, 1913 (report of Superintendent), and that he was unmarried and without surviving issue or parents at the time of his death. Had he died intestate, he would have left as heirs to his estate, which was solely personal in character, under the laws of distribution of New Mexico (Sec. 2034 Compiled Laws 1897) Lot Eyelash, brother, Michael (or Mike) Nantan, half-brother, and the husband and children of a *(illegible)* deceased daughter (Anne Gooday) of a previously deceased brother (E-zhi-ye), as follows: Gooday or Talbot (inheriting through Maurine Gooday), Annie or Amy Imach Enoha, Blossom Ha-o-zons, Irene, Bessie, Ida, Willie and Hilda Gooday.

It appears that the Gooday heirs have not testified at either of the hearings held in the case and that they did not receive notice thereof; however, since their interests have been in no way prejudiced by the omission, and the procuring of complete evidence appears to have been peculiarly difficult in this case, it is recommended that Departmental requirement of notice of hearing be waived.

Sam Binday was a tribal Indian who had never been allotted. A few days before his death, he stated to Eric Spitty and Eugene Chihuahua, according to their testimony, that he wished his property given to Horace Yahnahki, a cousin. The intention of the testator is further shown by the affidavits of Roger Toclanny, Horace Yahnahki, and Jasper Kanseah, and the report of the Superintendent strongly recommends approval of the verbal will on the ground that Sam Binday was a non-citizen Indian, and that the verbal will is a custom of the Apache tribe. This conclusion is concurred in my Major George W. Goode, formerly in charge of the Apache prisoners of war, in a report made November 29, 1913, and the opinion of E. H. Crowder, Judge Advocate General of the War Department, rendered December 11, 1913, and a part of the file in this case, is based upon such conclusion.

In pursuance of the opinion referred to above $1832.35, belonging to the estate of Sam Binday, were transferred on March 2, 1914, from the Office of the Apache prisoners of war at Fort Sill, Oklahoma, to the Superintendent of the Mescalero Agency, to the credit of Horace Yahnahki.

Even if Sam Binday were not a tribal, but a citizen Indian, his verbal will would be valid under the laws of New Mexico (Sections 1948, 1950, Compiled Laws of New Mexico, 1897).

Under the law and the regulations of the Department relative to the approval of Indian wills (except for the Five Civilized Tribes and the Osage Agency) no limitations are imposed on the Secretary of the Interior requiring him to observe the laws of any state; but it is the opinion of the Office in a case like the present one where the intention of the decedent to make a testamentary disposition of his property is clear and uncontroverted, and especially where, under a legal opinion previously rendered on full consideration (although not binding on account of lack of jurisdiction), the property has already been set apart to the legatee, the approval of such a will would be proper; and it is therefore respectfully recommended that the verbal will of Sam Binday, bequeathing his entire estate to Horace Yaknahki, be approved.

> Respectfully,
> *EB Meritt*

11-DEMC-12.   Assistant Commissioner.
Inclosure[sic] 1366

Department of The Interior
Office of The Secretary FEB 1 1916

Approved: *Bo Sweeney*
                                              Assistant Secretary

▲▼▲▼▲▼▲▼▲▼▲▼▲▼▲▼

SALLY BAKER

> OFFICE OF INDIAN AFFAIRS
> RECEIVED
> FEB 24 1912
> **18707**

LAST WILL AND TESTAMENT

OF

SALLY BAKER.

I, Sally Baker, being of sound mind and disposing memory, and of good health, but realizing the uncertainties of life, do hereby make, declare, and publish this my LAST WILL AND TESTAMENT as follows:

Indian Wills, 1911 – 1921 Book Three
Records of The Bureau of Indian Affairs

1ˢᵗ To my son, Charles Rave, I give, devise, and bequeath my allotment described as the west one half of the south east quarter of Sec. 29, Tp. 26 N. of Range 8 east of the sixth P. M. in Nebraska, containing 80 acres more or less according to the government survey.

       This will is drawn under the provisions of the Act of Congress of June 25th, 1910 and subject to the conditions that no sale or conveyance of the land described, by the devisee, his heirs, administrators, or legal representatives during the period of the trust, declared in the trust patent issued to me, Sally Baker, for said land shall be valid unless approved by the Secretary of the Interior.

John Rave   Sally Baker her [thumb print] mark
Witness to mark and interpreter.

The said testatrix at this time signed her name to the above and foregoing instrument in the presence of the undersigned and at the same time declared it to be her last will and testament and we, at her request and in her presence and in the presence of each other do hereby sign our names hereto as attesting witnesses.

               Albert Russell
               Harry Pelkey

Winnebago Agency, Nebraska,
February 21, 1912

Department of The Interior,
Office of Indian Affairs, Washington,
               OCT 19 1915
The within will of Sally Baker is recommended for approval in accordance with the Act of June 25, 1910 (36 Stats. L., 855-6) as amended by Act of February 14, 1913 (37 Stats. L., 678).

               Respectfully,
               (Signed)E.B.Meritt
               Assistant Commissioner
Department of The Interior
Office of The Secretary
          OCT 23 1915

Indian Wills, 1911 – 1921 Book Three
Records of The Bureau of Indian Affairs

The within will of Sally Baker is approved accordance with the Act of June 25, 1910 (36 Stats. L., 855-6) as amended by Act of February 14, 1913 (37 Stats. L., 678).

(Signed) Bo Sweeney
Assistant Secretary

▲▼▲▼▲▼▲▼▲▼▲▼▲▼▲▼

FRANK CANNON

LAST WILL AND TESTAMENT OF FRANK CANNON.

BE IT REMEMBERED THAT I, Frank Cannon, and[sic] Osage Indian of Osage county, state of Oklahoma, being in delicate health, but of sound and disposing mind; realizing the uncertainty of human life, do make this my LAST WILL AND TESTAMENT, in manner and form following; THAT IS TO SAY:

First:- I hereby revoke all other and former wills;

Second:- I, desire to be burried[sic] without pomp or ostentation, and that my debts including my funeral expenses and the expenses of my last illness also the expenses of writing this will, be paid with convenient haste out of any money available for any purpose;

Third:- I desire that Dr. J.G. Shoun be executor of this my last will to act without bond.

Fourth:- I, give, devise and bequeath to my brother Alex Cannon, the Two thirds of the rents, revenue and income from my homestead, the same being the SW.1/4, of Sec. 36, T.24, N.R.3, E.I.M. also one Rock Island buggy, One heating stove.
I desire that the remainder of my trust fund, be used to pay my just and legal debts, and if the same is not sufficient I desire that the rest of my debts be paid out of my annuity.

Fifth:- After all my debts are paid, I desire that the rest and residue of my annuity, royalty, bonus, rent premium or honorarium be equally divided between my wife Myrtle Cannon and my brother Alex Cannon.

Sixth:- I give, devise and bequeath to Gurney Miller One Dun horse about Seven years old:

Seventh:- I desire that one black horse about Six years old be sold, and the proceeds be paid to Charley Bigheart.

Eighth:- Of all the rest and residue of my estate both real, and personal, I give, devise and bequeath to my beloved wife Myrtle Cannon.

IN WITNESS WHEREOF, I Frank Cannon have hereunto set my hand, sealed, published and declared this to be my last will and testament, this 22nd, day of May One thousand Nine hundred Fifteen.

Frank Cannon

The foregoing instrument consisting of one sheet, was here and now signed by Frank Cannon, in our presence, and at his request, in his presence and in the presence of each other, we have signed as witnesses and he has published and declared this to be his Last will and testament.

WITNESSES.

Dlake Hublen	Residing at Fairfax Oklahoma.
Rose Hunkahoppy	Residing at Gray Horse, Oklahoma.
Lea Roberts	Residing at Gray Horse, Oklahoma.

Department of The Interior,
Office of Indian Affairs, Washington,
APR 28 1916
It is recommended that the within will be approved under the provisions of the Act of April 18, 1912 (37 Stat. 86, 88).

Respectfully,
(Signed)E.B.Meritt
Assistant Commissioner

Department of The Interior
Office of The Secretary

The within will is approved under the provisions of the Act of April 18, 1912 (37 Stat. 86, 88).

(No signature)
Assistant Secretary

EVA GOOD VOICE IRON

Original
WILL

OFFICE OF INDIAN AFFAIRS
RECEIVED
APR 19 1915
44371

OFFICE OF INDIAN AFFAIRS
RECEIVED
MAY 21 1915
56925

I, **Eva Good Voice Iron** of Pine Ridge Agency, South Dakota, Allottee number **6460** do hereby make and declare this to be my last will and testament, in accordance with Section 2 of the Act of June 25, 1910, (36 stat. 855-858) and Act of February 14, 1913, (Public No. 381), hereby revoking all former wills made by me:

1. I hereby direct that as soon as possible after my decease, that all my debts, funeral and testamentary expenses be paid out of my personal estate.

2. I give and devise my allotment on the Pine Ridge Reservation, South Dakota, described as follows:

E/2 of Sec. 19, T 36 N, R 44 W of 6th P. M., S. D.   320 acres

in the following manner:

NE/4 of Sec. 19, T 36 N, R 44 W, to my husband, Chas. Good Voice Iron

Ida
SE/4 of Sec. 19, T 36 N, R 44 W, to my grand child, ~~Cora~~ Bird Necklace.

3. I give and bequeath all of my personal property of whatsoever nature and wheresoever situated unto

4. All the rest of my property, real or personal, now possessed or hereafter acquired, of whatsoever nature and wheresoever situated, I hereby give, devise and bequeath unto

my husband, Chas. Good Voice Iron

(Property consists of one wagon and some household furniture)

In witness whereof I have hereunto set my hand this **2d** day of **April 1915.**   **her**
                                              Eva Good Voice Iron [thumb print]
                                                                    mark
        The above statement was, this **2d** day of **April 1915,** signed and published by **Eva Good Voice Iron** as **her** last will and testament, in the joint presence of the undersigned, the said **Eva Good Voice Iron** then being of sound and vigorous mid and free from any constraint or compulsion; whereupon we, being without any interest in the matter other than friendship, and being well acquainted with **her** but not members of **her** family, immediately subscribed our names hereto in the presence of each other and of the said testator, for the purpose of attesting the said will, as **she** requested us to do., **and that I, H.E. Wright, affixed her name in typewriting but that the testatrix placed her thumb mark thereon.**   Post Office Address
        H E Wright   **Pine Ridge, S. D.**
        OC Ross   **Pine Ridge, S. D.**

                                        Pine Ridge, South Dakota.
                                                April 12, 1915
        I hereby certify that I have fully inquired into the mental competency of the Indian signing the above will; the circumstances attending the execution of the will; the influence that may have induced its execution, and the names of those entitled to share in the estate under the law of descent in South Dakota: reasons for the disposition of the property proposed by the will differing from disposition had the property descended by operation of law.
        I respectfully forward this will with the recommendation that it be …..approved.
                                        John R Brennan
                                        Supt. & Spl. Disb. Agent.
Department of The Interior,
Office of Indian Affairs, Washington,

It is recommended that the within will be approved in accordance with the Act of June 25, 1910 (36 Stats. L., 855-6) as amended by Act of February 14, 1913 (37 Stats. L., 678).
                                        Respectfully,
                                        EB Meritt
                                        Assistant Commissioner
Department of The Interior JUN -7 1915

Office of The Secretary

The within will is hereby approved in accordance with the Act of June 25, 1910 (36 Stats. L., 855-6) as amended by Act of February 14, 1913 (37 Stats. L., 678).

Bo Sweeney
Assistant Secretary

ANTHONY HILTON

OFFICE OF INDIAN AFFAIRS RECEIVED AUG 5 1913 95568

OFFICE OF INDIAN AFFAIRS RECEIVED MAY 24 1915 57679

LAST WILL AND TESTAMENT

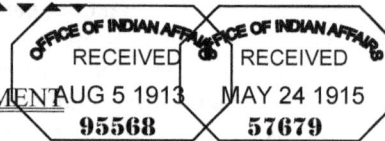

I, Anthony Hilton, of Anadarko, Caddo County, Oklahoma being now in good health, strength of body and mind, but sensible of the uncertainty of life and desiring to make disposition of my property and affairs while in health and strength, do hereby make and declare the following to be my last will and testament, hereby revoking and cancelling all other or former wills by me at any time made:

First. I direct the payment of all my just debts and funeral expenses.

Second. I give and devise to my beloved mother, To-co-me-me, who is Wichita allottee No. 619, all my property, real and personal, the real property consisting of my trust allotment known as Wichita allotment No. 620, which comprises the south-west quarter of Section seven, township seven north, range ten west (SW/4, 7-7N-10W). This will is made subject to the approval of the Secretary of the Interior.

In witness whereof I, Anthony Hilton, have to this my last will and testament, consisting of one sheet of paper, subscribed my name this thirty-first day of July, 1913.

Anthony Hilton

Subscribed by Anthony Hilton in the presence of each of us, the undersigned, and at the same time declared by him to us to be his last will and testament, and we, thereupon, at the request of Anthony Hilton, in his presence and in the presence of each other, sign our names hereto as witnesses, this 31st day of July, 1913, at Anadarko, Caddo county, Oklahoma.

Indian Wills, 1911 – 1921 Book Three
Records of The Bureau of Indian Affairs

(Signature Illegible)
P.O. *Anadarko, Okla.*
H.F. Bretshneider
P.O. *Anadarko, Okla*

Department of The Interior,
Office of Indian Affairs, Washington,
NOV -2 1915
It is recommended that the within will be approved in accordance with the provisions of the Act of June 25, 1910 (36 Stats. L., 855-6) as amended by Act of February 14, 1913 (37 Stats. L., 678).

Respectfully,
CF Hawke
Acting Assistant Commissioner

Department of The Interior
Office of The Secretary
NOV 12 1915
The within will is hereby approved in accordance with the provisions of the Act of June 25, 1910 (36 Stats. L., 855-6) as amended by Act of February 14, 1913 (37 Stats. L., 678).

Bo Sweeney
Assistant Secretary

▲▼▲▼▲▼▲▼▲▼▲▼

RED EARTH

Original WILL

OFFICE OF INDIAN AFFAIRS
RECEIVED
MAR -9 1914
25566

OFFICE OF INDIAN AFFAIRS
RECEIVED
NOV 23 1915
125897

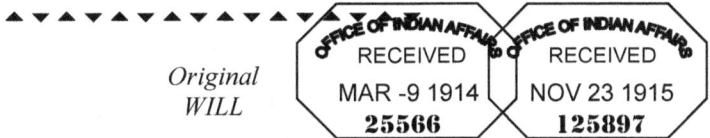

I, **Red Earth** of Pine Ridge Agency, South Dakota, Allottee number 1217 do hereby make and declare this to be my last will and testament, in accordance with Section 2 of the Act of June 25, 1910, (36 stat. 855-858) and Act of February 14, 1913, (Public No. 381), hereby revoking all former wills made by me:

1. I hereby direct that as soon as possible after my decease, that all my debts, funeral and testamentary expenses be paid out of my personal estate.

2. I give and devise my allotment on the Pine Ridge Reservation, South Dakota, described as follows:

E/2 of Sec. 28, T36, R 48

in the following manner:

NE/4 of Sec. 28, T 36, R 48 to Mrs. Lucy Shangreau, or in case this land has been sold the proceeds shall go to Mrs. Lucy Shangreau.

SE/4 of Sec. 28, T 36, R 48 to Louis Shangreau.

3. ~~I give and bequeath all of my personal property of whatsoever nature and wheresoever situated unto~~ *(Marked out on microfilm.)*

4.   All the rest of my property, real or personal, now possessed or hereafter acquired, of whatsoever nature and wheresoever situated, I hereby give, devise and bequeath unto

Louis Shangreau

In witness whereof I have hereunto set my hand this **26th** day of **February** 1914.   *her*
Red Earth [thumb print]
mark

The above statement was, this **26th** day of **February** 1914 signed and published by **Red Earth** as **her** last will and testament, in the joint presence of the undersigned, the said **Red Earth** then being of sound and vigorous mid and free from any constraint or compulsion; whereupon we, being without any interest in the matter other than friendship, and being well acquainted with **her** but not members of **her** family, immediately subscribed our names hereto in the presence of each other and of the said testator, for the purpose of attesting the said will, as **she** requested us to do.

Post Office Address
John Fool head   **Pine Ridge, S. D.**
Robert A.O Bear   **Pine Ridge, S. D.**

Pine Ridge, South Dakota.
Mar -2 1914
I hereby certify that I have fully inquired into the mental competency of the Indian signing the above will; the circumstances attending the execution of the will; the influence that may have induced

its execution, and the names of those entitled to share in the estate under the law of descent in South Dakota: reasons for the disposition of the property proposed by the will differing from disposition had the property descended by operation of law.

I respectfully forward this will with the recommendation that it be …..approved.

John R Brennan
Supt. & Spl. Disb. Agent.

Department of The Interior,
Office of Indian Affairs, Washington,
NOV 11 1914

The within will of Red Earth is recommended for approval in accordance with the provisions of the Act of June 25, 1910 (36 Stats. L., 855-6) as amended by Act of February 14, 1913 (37 Stats. L., 678).

Respectfully,
E B Meritt
Acting Assistant Commissioner

Department of The Interior
Office of The Secretary NOV 12 1914

The within will of Red Earth is approved in accordance with the Act of June 25, 1910 (36 Stats. L., 855-6) as amended by Act of February 14, 1913 (37 Stats. L., 678).

Bo Sweeney
Assistant Secretary

▲▼▲▼▲▼▲▼▲▼▲▼▲▼▲▼

HOARSE VOICE

> OFFICE OF INDIAN AFFAIRS
> RECEIVED
> SEP 25 1915
> **103763**

In The Name of God, Amen.

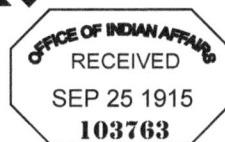

I, Hoarse Voice, of Kingfisher, Kingfisher County, Oklahoma, of the age of 75 years, being now in fair health strength and clear in mind, but sensible of the uncertainty of life and the certainty of death, and desiring to make disposition of my property and affairs while in health and strength, do hereby make, publish, and declare the following to be my

LAST WILL AND TESTAMENT.

Indian Wills, 1911 – 1921 Book Three
Records of The Bureau of Indian Affairs

1st   I give, devise and bequeath to my Grand-Niece, Inez Midnight, 35 years of age, and present wife of John Bull, all my real estate and allotment No. 489, described as the North-east quarter (1/4) of Section Fourteen (14), Township fifteen (15), North of Range eight (8) West I. M., containing 160 acres of land, to her and her heirs forever.

2nd   I also bequeath to said Inez Midnight, one brown mule about fourtee[sic] years old; one lumber wagon, and one double harness.

3rd   I also devise and bequeath to her, Inez Midnight, any and all personal property of which I may die possessed, and direct the paymet[sic] of all my just debts and funeral expenses..

    In witness whereof I have hereunto set my hand this 11th day of May, 1914.   *her*
                                             Hoarse Voice [thumb print]
In presence of:-   *mark*
        DeWitt Hayes
        Robert Burns

    Subscribed by Hoarse Voice in the presence of us, the undersigned, and declared by her to be her Last Will and Testament and at the request of Hoarse Voice, in her presence, and in the presence of each other, sign our names as witnesses hereto this 11th day of May, 1914, Robert Burns acting as Interpreter and Hoarse Voice declaring she fully understands the report of said will.
                                        Robert Burns
                                        DeWitt C Hayes
                                        Lida H Barnes
Department of The Interior,
Office of Indian Affairs, Washington,
                    NOV 27 1915
It is recommended that the within will be approved pursuant to the provisions of the Act of June 25, 1910 (36 Stats. L., 855-6) as amended by Act of February 14, 1913 (37 Stats. L., 678).
                                        Respectfully,
                                        E B Meritt
                                        Acting Assistant Commissioner
Department of The Interior
Office of The Secretary NOV 29 1915

The within will is hereby approved pursuant to the provisions of the Act of June 25, 1910 (36 Stats. L., 855-6) as amended by Act of February 14, 1913 (37 Stats. L., 678).

Bo Sweeney
Assistant Secretary

▲▼▲▼▲▼▲▼▲▼▲▼▲▼▲▼

MOO CHO ROOK

WILL

I, Moo cho rook, Comanche Indian allottee No. 2307, of Comanche County, Oklahoma, sound of mind and body but sensible of the uncertainty of of[sic] life and desiring to make disposition of my property and affairs while in good health and strength, do hereby make and declare the following to be my last will and testament, hereby revoking all other or former wills be[sic] me at any time made.

First.   I desire the payment of all my just debts and funeral expenses.

Second.   I give and devise to *D*ro haw wah, Comanche Indian allottee No. 2308, my wife, all of the following:

My trust allotment of land, No. 2307 and covering the SE/4, 31-1N-13W;

All my interest in Comanche allotment No. 2013, covering the SE/4, 5-1S-13W, of which allotment I was adjudged one-half heir by the Department of the Interior, as is evidenced by its letter "Land-Sales 244-1912;[sic]

All of my stock, money and any other property belonging to me at my death.

This will is made subject to the approval of the Secretary of the Interior.

In witness whereof, I, Moo cho rook, have to this, my last will and testament, consisting of ~~one~~*two* sheet*s* of paper, subscribed my name this *11th* day of *December, 1913.*

77

Moo cho rook

Subscribed by Moo cho rook, the testator in the presence of each of us, the undersigned, and at the same time declared by him to us to be his last will and testament, and we, thereupon, at the request of the testator, Moo-cho rook, in his presence and in the presence of each other, sign our names hereto, as witnesses this *11th* day of *December* 1913, at *home* near Cache, Comanche County, Oklahoma.

Department of The Interior,
Office of Indian Affairs, Washington,

It is recommended that the within will be approved pursuant to the provisions of the Act of June 25, 1910 (36 Stats. L., 855-6) as amended by Act of February 14, 1913 (37 Stats. L., 678).

Respectfully,
EB Meritt
Assistant Commissioner

Department of The Interior
Office of The Secretary

The within will is approved pursuant to the provisions of the Act of June 25, 1910 (36 Stats. L., 855-6) as amended by Act of February 14, 1913 (37 Stats. L., 678).

(Signed) Bo Sweeney
Assistant Secretary

GOOD WOMAN BLACK EAGLE

-WILL-

OFFICE OF INDIAN AFFAIRS
RECEIVED
SEP 28 1914
104076

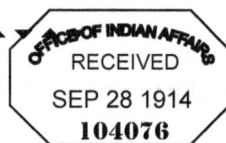

IN THE NAME OF GOD: AMEN: I, Good woman Black eagle, being of sound mind, but infirm body, do hereby and by these presents, make, declare and publish this to be my last will and testament.

1st.   I hereby give, devise and bequeath, unto James Garfield, Jr., my grazing allotment, described as the N/2 of Sec. 11, Township 27 North, Range 46 East of the Montana Meridian, Montana, in consideration of the many kindnesses he has shown to me.

2nd. I hereby give, devise and bequeath, unto Nellie Smith, of Wolf Point, Montana, my irrigable allotment, described as the Southeast quarter of the Southwest quarter (SE/4 of SW/4) of Section twentyseven[sic] (27), Township twentyseven[sic] (27) North, Range ofrtysix[sic] (46) East of the Montana Meridian, Montana, in consideration of the many kindnesses she has shown to me.

IN WITNESS WHEREOF, I have hereunto set my hand, this *31* day of *August*, in the year 1914.

her
GOOD WOMAN BLACK EAGLE [thumb print]
mark.

We, the undersigned, hereby certify that we were present at, and witnessed the signing by Good woman Black eagle, of the above will, and that she signed the same in the presence of each of us, and that she declared the same to be her last will and testament, and that we have signed this will as witnesses in the presence of each other and in the presence of the testator, on the day and year last above written.

Clyde Patton
Isaac Blount

Department of The Interior,
Office of Indian Affairs, Washington,
JUL -6 1915

It is recommended that the within will be disapproved pursuant to the provisions of the Act of June 25, 1910 (36 Stats. L., 855-6) as amended by Act of February 14, 1913 (37 Stats. L., 678).

Respectfully,
(Signed) *EB Meritt*
Assistant Commissioner

Department of The Interior
Office of The Secretary

The within will is hereby disapproved pursuant to the provisions of the Act of June 25, 1910 (36 Stats. L., 855-6) as amended by Act of February 14, 1913 (37 Stats. L., 678).

A A Jones
First Assistant Secretary

▲ ▼ ▲ ▼ ▲ ▼ ▲ ▼ ▲ ▼ ▲ ▼ ▲ ▼ ▲ ▼

JOB LONGEAR

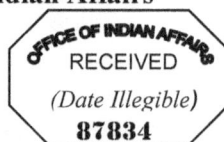

Last Will and testament of Job Longear.

OFFICE OF INDIAN AFFAIRS
RECEIVED
(Date Illegible)
87834

Job Longear, being of sound mind and memory, hereby declares and publish[sic], this my last will and testament:

First: I give and bequeath to my grand-daughter, Bella Longear, SW/4 of the NW/4 of Section Twenty-six (26) Township Ninety-four (94) North of Range Sixty-two (62), and all the buildings on this land to go to her after my death.

Second: I give and bequeath to my grand-son, James Longear, the North West quarter of the North West quarter of Section (26) Twenty-six, Township Ninety-four (94) North of Range Sixty-two (62) containing 40 acres.

Third: I give and bequeath to my Grand-daughter, Fidelia Longear, the North Eat quarter of the North east quarter of Section Twenty-seven (27) Township Ninety-four (94) North of Range Sixty-two (62), containing 40 acres.

Fourth: I give and bequeath to my grand-daughter, Rebecca Longear, the South East quarter of the North East quarter of Section Twenty-seven (27) Township Ninety-four (94) North of Range Sixty-two (62) containing 40 acres.

Fifth: I give and bequeath to my four Grand-children, Bella James, Fidelia and Rebecca Longear all the money I have deposited to my credit at the Yankton Agency, each child to share equally.

Sixth: I hereby appoint Charles Longear as executor to this my last Will and testament and give him power to act as such.   his
Interpreter: JOB LONGEAR [thumb print]
  Moses Archancheau   mark

Signed, sealed and declared by the said Job Longear as and for his last Will and testament in presence of us, who at his request and in his presence and in the presence of each other, have subscribed our names as witnesses hereto.

Indian Wills, 1911 – 1921 Book Three
Records of The Bureau of Indian Affairs

W.B. McCown   Residing at Greenwood, South Dakota.
Moses Archancheau Residing at Greenwood, South Dakota.

Job Longear, being first duly sworn according to law deposes and says: That he has on this day made a Will leaving all of his property, Personal and Real to his four Grandchildren, namely- Bella, James, Fidelia and Rebecca Longear. That he has four living children of his own who would of inherited this land but he wish it to go to these Grandchildren. That all of his children have allotments of his[sic] own and his grandchildren have none and he wishes these children to make their home on this land. That he has other Grand-children living but he picked on these four grand-children to have this land and he wishes it to be divided this way. The father of these four children have always taken care of me and that I have always lived with him.

Witnesses: JOB LONGEAR [thumb print]
   Moses Archancheau   mark
   WB McCown
   Greenwood, SD

Subscribed and sworn to before me this 19th day of May 1913.

                    W.B. McCown
                    Notary Public.

My Commission expires 12/24/16.

Department of The Interior,   OCT 21 1915
Office of Indian Affairs, Washington,
It is recommended that the within will be approved pursuant to the provisions of the Act of June 25, 1910 (36 Stats. L., 855-6) as amended by Act of February 14, 1913 (37 Stats. L., 678).

                    Respectfully,
                    EB Meritt
                    Assistant Commissioner

Department of The Interior
Office of The Secretary
         OCT 22 1915
The within will is hereby approved pursuant to the provisions of the Act of June 25, 1910 (36 Stats. L., 855-6) as amended by Act of February 14, 1913 (37 Stats. L., 678).

Bo Sweeney
Assistant Secretary

▲▼▲▼▲▼▲▼▲▼▲▼▲▼

RECEIVED

OCT -7 1915

108249

JENNIE TICHENOR

In the name of God, Amen. Know all men, Taht[sic] I Jennie Tichenor of Curry County in the State of Oregon, of the age of about 67 years, being of sound and disposing mind and memory, and not acting under duress, menace, fraud or undue influence of any person whomsoever, do make, publish and delcare[sic] this my last Will and Testament in manner and form following, to-wit; First; It is my will, and I do order, that all my just debts and funeral expenses be duly paid and satisfied as soon as can be conveniently done after my decease. Second; I given[sic] and bequeath unto A E Hastings one horse and calf; to Lizzie Meservey one cow; to A E Hastings enough for two beds; to A.E. Hastings 1/2 the dishes and 1/2 the chairs the other 1/2 the dishes and chairs to Mrs. Elisha Meservey; to Elisha Meservey (boy) the bed in the SE room of the house in which I now live; one large kettel[sic] to Ada Meservey;

The proceeds from the sale of my allotment claim to be divided equally among George Meservey, Elisha Meservey, Ran Meservey, Hick Meservey, Ona Fry, Rosella Fry, Lizzie Meservey, Irene Meservey, Frankie Meservey, Tootsie Meservey, Lillian Meservey, Elisha Meservey Jr, Teddy Meservey, and A.E. Hastings, provided first that my doctor bills and funeral expenses and other debts are first satisfied out of the proceeds of said sale. I hereby select A.S. Miller as my executor to carry out the above described will. And lastly I nominate, constitute and appoint A.S. Miller to be the executor of this my last Will, hereby revoking all other Wills, legacies and bequests by me heretofore made, and declaring this, and no other, to be my last Will and Testament.

In witness whereof, I have hereunto set my hand, this 25th day of April in the year of our Lord One Thousand Nine Hundred and fourteen (14).

her

Jennie   X   Tichenor

mark.

The above instrument was at the date thereof signed, sealed and published and declared, by the said Jennies[sic] Tichenor as and for her

Last Will and Testament, in the presence of us, who, at her request and in her presence, and in the presence of each other, have subscribed our names as witnesses thereto.

A S Miller residing at near Wedderburn, Frank VanCamp residing at *(no other information given).*

The above Will was recorded the 12th day of May, 1914, in Book One of Wills at page 97 thereof.

Charges for making this copy 75 cents.

STATE OF OREGON,
> *ss.*

County of Curry,   I, **J.R.Stannard**   , *County Clerk and Clerk of the* **County** *Court of the County and State aforesaid, do hereby certify that the foregoing copy of* **Will of Jennie Tichenor, deceased.** *has been by me compared with the original, and that it is a correct transcript therefrom, and of the whole of such original* **Will** *as the same appears* **of record** *at my office and in my custody.*

In Testimony Whereof, I have hereunto set my hand and affixed the seal of said Court this **5th** *day of* **November** *1914.*

By *J. R. Stannard*
Clerk.

Department of The Interior,
Office of Indian Affairs, Washington, OCT 21 1915

It is recommended that the within will be approved under the provisions of the Act of June 25, 1910 (36 Stats. L., 855-6) as amended by Act of February 14, 1913 (37 Stats. L., 678) insofar as it relates to trust property.

EB Meritt
Assistant Commissioner

Department of The Interior
Office of The Secretary OCT 22 1915

The within will is approved pursuant to the provisions of the Act of June 25, 1910 (36 Stats. L., 855-6) as amended by Act of February 14, 1913 (37 Stats. L., 678) insofar as it relates to trust property.

Bo Sweeney
Assistant Secretary

▲ ▼ ▲ ▼ ▲ ▼ ▲ ▼ ▲ ▼ ▲ ▼ ▲ ▼ ▲ ▼

MOH-E-KAH-MOIE or MARY STEPSON

OFFICE OF INDIAN AFFAIRS
RECEIVED
OCT 22 1915
113220

LAST WILL AND TESTAMENT OF MON-E-KAH-MOIE,
ALIAS MARY STEPSON.

=

Be it remembered that I *Mary* Moh-e-kah-moie, Alias Mary Stepson, an Indian, residing at Gray Horse Osage County state of Oklahoma, being in a delicate state of health, but of sound and disposing mind; realizing the uncertainty of human life, do make this my last will and testament, in manner and form following; that is to say;

FIRST:- I hereby revoke all other and former wills:

SECOND:- I desire to be buried without pomp or ostentation, and that all of my legal debts, including my funeral expenses, the expenses of my last illness and the expense of writing this and a former will, be paid with convenient haste, out of any money that may be available for such purposes:

THIRD:- I desire that D.A. Shoun be made executor of this my last will and testament, to serve without bond:

FOURTH:- I Give, devise and bequeath, to William Stepson, a one third of all my Real Estate and money due to me or that may hereafter become due from rents, royalty and bonus, including my Trust Fund:

FIFTH:- I Give, devise and bequeath, to my mother, Hlu-ah-to-me, all of my personal effects including, household furniture, pictures, and all and every class and character of my individual and personal effects:

SIXTH:- I Give, devise and bequeath, to my daughter, Hlu-ah-to-me alias Mertie Stepson, all of the rest and residue of my estate both real and personal:

SEVENTH:- I desire that my mother, Hlu-ah-to-me, may be custodian of my daughter, Hlu-ah-to-me, alias Mertie Stepson, and that she have care and custody of her until she becomes of age under the laws of the State of Oklahoma.

IN WITNESS WHEREOF, I, Moh-e-kah-moie, alias Mary Stepson, have hereunto set my hand, sealed, published and declared this to be my last will and testament, this *5th* day of July, in the year of our Lord, One thousand nine hundred and fifteen.

her

Mary Moh e koh moie [thumb print]

WITNESSES.   *Mary Stepson*   *mark*
    Sam W Tulk
    Mamie Warrior
    Wm Stepson

ATTESTATION.

The foregoing instrument, consisting of one sheer, was here and now signed by *Mary* Moh-e-kah-moie, Alias Mary Stepson, in our presence; in her presence at her request, in her presence and in the presence of each other, we have signed as witnesses and she has published and declared this to be her last Will and Testament.

           :Sam W Tulk   Residing at, *Grayhorse Okla.*
WITNESSES.   *:Wm Stepson*   Residing at, *Gray Horse OK*
           :Mamie Warrior Residing at, *Pawhuska Okla*

I, the undersigned, signed the name of *Mary* Moh-e-kah-moie, (Mary Stepson) Osage allottee No. 121, to her will at her request and in her presence and witnesses her mark.

Sam W. Tulk

I, the undersigned, do hereby certify that I fully and truthfully interpreted and explained the foregoing will and testament to *Mary* Moh-e-kah-moie (Mary Stepson), Osage allottee No. 121, and I am satisfied that she clearly understood the nature of the provisions of the same and all the terms thereof.

Witness my hand at Grayhorse, Oklahoma, this *6th* day of *July* 1915.

Mamie Warrior

Department of The Interior,
Office of Indian Affairs, Washington, OCT 25 1915

Indian Wills, 1911 – 1921 Book Three
Records of The Bureau of Indian Affairs

The within will is respectfully recommended for approval pursuant to the provisions of the Act of April 18, 1912 (37 Stat. 87, 88).

Respectfully,
EB Meritt
Assistant Commissioner

Department of The Interior
Office of The Secretary OCT 26 1915

The within will is hereby approved pursuant to the provisions of the Act of April 18, 1912 (37 Stat. 87, 88).

Bo Sweeney
Assistant Secretary

▲ ▼ ▲ ▼ ▲ ▼ ▲ ▼ ▲ ▼ ▲ ▼ ▲ ▼ ▲ ▼

THOMAS DEAFSOLDIER

LAST WILL AND TESTAMENT of THOMAS DEAFSOLDIER.

IN THE NAME OF GOD AMEN.

I Thomas Deafsoldier of the State of South Dakota and County of Charles Mix, being of sound mind and memory but being uncertain of life and certain of the approach of death, and desiring to dispose of all my worldly possessions while I still have the power to do so, do make and declare this to be my last will and testament, hereby revoking and annulling any and all wills heretofore made by me.

First, I bequeath to my grandniece Margery Reed French that portion of my allotment described as follows Lots numbered 1083 and 1088 according to the survey of the Yankton Reservation.

Second, I also bequeath to my grandniece Margery Reed French all furniture and private effects belonging in my present dwelling house, also a light two horse wagon now in my possession.

Third, I bequeath to the heirs of my deceased wife, Nancy Deafsoldier, after waiving my own rights thereto, all the property belonging to her at the time of her death, including any inherited interests she may have had.

Fourth, I bequeath to my grand nephew Stephen Reed the buggy I now own, also 1 set of light buggy harness.

Fifth, I bequeath to Lytle French 1 set of double harness.

Sixth, I bequeat[sic] to James Reed, Albion Hitika, John Lowe and Eugene Bull, each to share alike, all moneys held in trust for me by the United States, after all my just debts and funeral expenses are paid and a monument erected at my grave to cost $200.

Seventh, I bequeath all the remainder of my property both real and personal, including any inherited interests I may have, to my leagal[sic] heirs. This includes Lots Nos. 1063 and 1066 and Lots 1081 and 1090 my deceased daughters[sic] allotment, according to the survey of the Yankton Reservation.

Intestimony[sic] hereof, I have set my hand and seal this 26th day of August 1915 at Greenwood, Charles Mix County, S.D.

His

Thomas Deafsoldier. [thumb print]

Mark

Signed, sealed published and declared this 26 day of August, 1915, by the said Thomas Deafsoldier, in our presence, as and for his last will and testament, and at his request and in his presence and in the presence of eachother[sic] we have here unto subscribed our names as attesting witnesses,

William Bourissour   *John McBride*   *(Signature Illegible)*

Department of The Interior,
Office of Indian Affairs, Washington,
                    FEB 10 1916
It is recommended that the within will be approved pursuant to the provisions of the Act of June 25, 1910 (36 Stats. L., 855-6) as amended by Act of February 14, 1913 (37 Stats. L., 678).

Respectfully,

EB Meritt

Assistant Commissioner

Department of The Interior
Office of The Secretary   FEB 17 1916

The within will is hereby approved pursuant to the provisions of the Act of June 25, 1910 (36 Stats. L., 855-6) as amended by Act of February 14, 1913 (37 Stats. L., 678).

Bo Sweeney
Assistant Secretary

▲▼▲▼▲▼▲▼▲▼▲▼▲▼

JOSHUA LOUIE

OFFICE OF INDIAN AFFAIRS
RECEIVED
MAR 1- 1915
33946

LAST WILL OF JOSHUA LOUIE

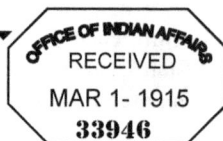

Be it remembered that I Joshua Louie of Siletz, Oregon, being of sound mind and memory do hereby make and declare the following as my last will and testament.

I give and bequeath to my three grandchildren, Norman Strong, Ruby Metcalf, and Ira Strong, each the Sum of Two Dollars.

I give and bequeath to Sissy Fuller, wife of Louie Fuller, the Sum of One Hundred Dollars.

I give and bequeath to my daughter, Minnie Lane, wife of Scott Lane of Siletz, Oregon, the remainder of my property, whether moneys, credits, real or personal wherever situated and of what ever nature for her use and benefit or in the event of her death before my death to her heirs.

Witness my hand and seal this fourth day of February, 1915.His right
Joshua Louie [thumb print]
Thumb Mark.

WITNESSES:
Chas H Goodner Merchant
Toledo, Oregon
Arthur Bensell Farmer
Siletz, Oregon

Signed, sealed, published and declared by Joshua Louie as and for his last will and testament in our presence and in the presence of each of us. And the said Joshua Louie is full age of sound and disposing mind and memory.

Chas H Goodner ⟨Seal⟩

WITNESSES: Toledo, Oregon.

Indian Wills, 1911 – 1921 Book Three
Records of The Bureau of Indian Affairs

Arthur Bensell
Siletz, Oregon. ⧆*Seal*

Department of The Interior,
Office of Indian Affairs, Washington,
APR 14 1915

The within will is respectfully recommended for approval pursuant to the provisions of the act of February 14, 1913 (37 Stat. L., 678).

EB Meritt
Assistant Commissioner

Department of The Interior
Office of The Secretary APR 17 1915

The within will is hereby approved, pursuant to the provisions of the Act of February 14, 1913 (37 Stat. L., 678).

Bo Sweeney
Assistant Secretary

▲▼▲▼▲▼▲▼▲▼▲▼▲▼▲▼

ME-PE DICK

In the Name of God, Amen.

I, **Me-pe Dick** , of *(No information given) in the County of* **Thurston**, *State of* **Nebraska**, *being of sound mind and memory, and considering the uncertainty of this frail and transitory life, do therefore make, ordain, publish and declare this to be my last* **Will and Testament:**

FIRST, *I order and direct that my Executor hereinafter named, pay all my just debts and funeral expenses as soon after my decease as conveniently may be.*

SECOND, *After the payment of such funeral expenses and debts, I give, devise and bequeath* **To my son Joseph Dick, my grand son Henry Clay, my grand son Logan Dick, and my grand daughters Margaret Dick and Susan Dick all of my own allotment of land to-wit The north west quarter of the south-west quarter, (NW1/4 of SW1/4) of section twenty seven in township twenty five, north of range eight, east of the sixth P.M. in Thurston County**

89

Nebraska, to have and to hold the same share and share alike, The legatees named being my children and the child of my deceased daughter Lucy Dick Clay, and of my son Joseph Dick,

LASTLY, I make, constitute and appoint **Joseph Dick** *to be Executor of this my last Will and Testament, hereby revoking all former Wills by me made.*

IN WITNESS WHEREOF, I have hereunto subscribed my name and affixed my seal, the **4th** *day of* **March** *in the year of our Lord, one thousand nine hundred* **fourteen**

her

Me-pe X Dick   Seal

mark

This Instrument was on the day of the date thereof, signed, published and declared by the said testator to be her last Will and Testament, in the presence of us who at her request have subscribed our names thereto as witnesses in her presence and in the presence of each other.

J. R. Ashley

W. J. Stephenson

Department of The Interior,
Office of Indian Affairs, Washington,

JAN 31 1916

It is recommended that the within will be approved pursuant to the provisions of the Act of June 25, 1910 (36 Stats. L., 855-6) as amended by Act of February 14, 1913 (37 Stats. L., 678).

EB Meritt

Assistant Commissioner

Department of The Interior
Office of The Secretary   FEB -1 1916

The within will is hereby approved pursuant to the provisions of the Act of June 25, 1910 (36 Stats. L., 855-6) as amended by Act of February 14, 1913 (37 Stats. L., 678).

Bo Sweeney

Assistant Secretary

▲▼▲▼▲▼▲▼▲▼▲▼▲▼

<u>WA-TON-NE MITCHELL</u>

W I L L

I, Wa-ton-ne Mitchell, of the Omaha tribe of Indians, and a resident of Thurston County, Nebraska, being of sound mind and memory, do hereby and by these presents, make publish and declare this instrument to be my last will and testament, hereby revoking any former will, which I may have made.

FIRST.

I give and bequeath and devise unto my husband, Arthur Mitchell, his heirs, the SW/4 of the NW/4, of Section 5, Township 25 N., Range 9 East, of the 6th P.M., containing 40 acres.

SECOND

I give and bequeath and devise unto my sister, Daisy Walker, her heirs, the SE/4 of the NW/4, of Section 5, Township 25 North, Range 9 East, of the 6th P.M., containing 40 acres.

THIRD

I give and bequeath and devise unto my husband, Arthur Mitchell, his heirs, all money of which I may be possessed of at the time of my death held in trust by the Superintendent of the Omaha Indian Agency.

IN WITNESS WHEREOF I have hereunto set my hand this 21st day of May, 1915, in the presence of:- *Her mark*

Wa-ton-ne Mitchell [thumb print]

Witnesses:
Silas Wood
Silas White

We, the undersigned, do hereby certify that we have signed the above instrument as subscribing witnesses in the presence of each other and at her request and said instrument was explained to said testator in our presence and she understood the same, and and[sic] said testator did thereupon sign the same.

Witnesses:
Silas Wood

Silas White

SUBSCRIBED and SWORN to before me this 21st day of May, 1915.

Axel Johnson
Superintendent, Omaha Indian Agency

Department of The Interior,
Office of Indian Affairs, Washington,
JAN 25 1916

It is recommended that the within will be approved in pursuance of the provisions of the Act of June 25, 1910 (36 Stats. L., 855-6) as amended by Act of February 14, 1913 (37 Stats. L., 678).

Respectfully,
EB Meritt
Assistant Commissioner

Department of The Interior
Office of The Secretary   JAN 25 1916

The within will is hereby approved in pursuance of the provisions of the Act of June 25, 1910 (36 Stats. L., 855-6) as amended by Act of February 14, 1913 (37 Stats. L., 678).

Bo Sweeney
Assistant Secretary

▲▼▲▼▲▼▲▼▲▼▲▼▲▼

KO-YANT

OFFICE OF INDIAN AFFAIRS
RECEIVED
NOV 5- 1915
118490

WILL.

Mountain View, Oklahoma.
June 14, 1915

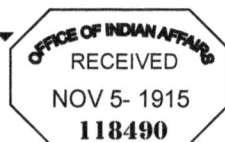

I, Ko-yant, Kiowa Indian allottee No. 669, of *Mtn View*, Kiowa County, Oklahoma, being now in good health, strength of body and mind, but sensible of the uncertainty of live[sic], and desiring to make disposition of my property and affairs while in health and strength, do hereby make, publish and declare the following to be my last will and testament, hereby revoking and cancelling all other or former wills by me at any time made.

First: I direct the payment of all my just debts and funeral expenses.

Indian Wills, 1911 – 1921 Book Three
Records of The Bureau of Indian Affairs

Second: I give and devise to my beloved daughter, Tah-ko-poodle, (Susie) Kiowa Indian allottee No. 671, the following real property to-wit: The North East Quarter, Section Eight (8), Township Seven (7) North, Range Fourteen (14) West of the Indian Meridian, in Kiowa County, Oklahoma, being known upon the rolls of the Interior Department as Kiowa Indian allotment No. 673, allotted to To-quoot, deceased.

Third: I give and devise to my beloved grand daughter, Tone-ke-ah-bo, Kiowa Indian allottee No. 2518, the following real property, to-wit: The North West Quarter (4) Section Eight (8) Township Seven (7) North Range Fourteen (14) West of the Indian Meridian in Kiowa County, Oklahoma, being known upon the rolls of the Interior Department as Kiowa Indian allotment No. 1007, allotted to Pe-ah-ke-a-dah, deceased; and the West half of the North West of Section Seventeen (17) Township Seven (7) North, Range Fourteen (14) West of the Indian Meridian in Kiowa County, Oklahoma, being a part of Kiowa Indian allotment No. 670, allotted to my deceased wife, A-day-pay-bah.

Fourth: I give and devise to my beloved grand daughter, Eunice Tone-ke-ah-bo, Kiowa Indian allottee No. 2883, the following real property, to-wit: The South East Quarter, Section Five (5) Township Seven (7) North, Range Fourteen (14) West of the Indian Meridian in Kiowa County, Oklahoma, being known upon the rolls of the Interior Department as Kiowa allotment No. 669, being my own allotment.

Five: I give and decree all the rest, residue and remainder of all other property, real and personal, of which I may die possessed, to the following persons, in equal shares:

Tah-ko-poodle, daughter, who is Kiowa Indian allottee No. 671
Eliza Tone-ke-ah-bo, grand daughter, who is Kiowa Indian allottee No. 2518
Eunice Tone-ke-ah-bo, grand daughter, who is Kiowa Indian allottee No. 2885
Ed Ko-yant grand son, who is Kiowa Indian allottee No. 3331

This will is made subject to the approval of the Secretary of the Interior.

In witness whereof, I, Ko-yant, Kiowa Indian allottee No. 669, have

93

to this my last will and testament consisting of ~~two~~ *three* sheets of paper, subscribe my name this *14th* day of *June* , 1915.　　　　　　　 his thumb

　　　　　　　　　　　　　　　　　　　　　Ko-yant [thumb print]

Witnesses.　　　　　　　　　　　　　　　　　　　　　　　　 mark

　　Ralph Ahpeatone

　　Enos Haumko

Subscribed by Ko-yant, Kiowa Indian allottee No. 669, in the presence of each of us, the undersigned, and at the same time declared by him to us to be his last will and testament, and we, thereupon, at the request of Ko-yant, in his presence and in the presence of each other, sign our names hereto as witnesses this *14* day of *June*, 1915 at _____ Kiowa County, Oklahoma.

Ralph Ahpeatone

STATEMENT AS TO HEIRSHIP.

I, Ko-yant, Kiowa Indian allottee No. 669, who made a will this day devising of certain trust property as shown in the will itself, hereby make the following statement concerning persons who are related to me, and who would, in the event of my decease, be entitled to share in my estate. At this time I also desire to state that Eliza Tone-ke-ah-bo, my grand daughter, has cared for me a long time and it is for that reason that I think that it is not more than just that she receive a good share of my estate after my death:

My wife, A-dau-pau-nah, Kiowa Indian allottee No. 670 is dead. I have only one child living at this time, and her name is Tah-ko-poodle, who is Kiowa Indian allottee No. 671. There are two children of my deceased son, Tone-ke-ah-bo living at this time, and their names are Eliza Tone-ke-ah-bo, Kiowa Indian allottee No. 2518; and Eunice Tone0ke-ah-bo Kiowa Indian allottee No. 2885. Besides these grand children Ed Ko-yant, Kiowa Indian allottee No. 333 is living at this time, he being the son of Ko-au-de-ah, who was otherwise known as John Ko-yant, who was my son, and who died November 22, 1907.

There are no other grand children besides the three enumerated above living, nor are there any other members of the tribe related to me, and entitled to share in my estate, in the event of my decease.

Signed this *14* day of *June* , 1915.
                        his thumb

                                        Ko-yant[thumb print]
Witnesses.   Allottee.
    Ralph Ahpeatone
    Enos Haumko

                            P.O. *Cornegie Okla.*
                            Enos Haumko
                            P.O. *Mt. View Okla.*

INTERPRETER'S CERTIFICATE.

I, Jasper Saun-ka-ah, a Kiowa Indian, hereby certify that I acted as interpreter during the execution of the foregoing will and testament made by Ko-yant; that I fully interpreted the foregoing will to him; that the same is fully understood by him, and that the same was drawn up in accordance with his directions and desires; that I have no interest in this matter, and that I speak both the Kiowa Indian and the English languages fluently.

Signed this *14th* day of *June*, 1915.

                            Jasper Saunkaah
                            Interpreter.

Department of The Interior,
Office of Indian Affairs, Washington,
                DEC -2 1915
It is recommended that the within will be approved pursuant to the provisions of the Act of June 25, 1910 (36 Stats. L., 855-6) as amended by Act of February 14, 1913 (37 Stats. L., 678).

                            Respectfully,
                            EB Meritt
                            Assistant Commissioner
Department of The Interior
Office of The Secretary   DEC -6 1915

The within will is hereby approved pursuant to the provisions of the Act of June 25, 1910 (36 Stats. L., 855-6) as amended by Act of February 14, 1913 (37 Stats. L., 678).

Indian Wills, 1911 – 1921 Book Three
Records of The Bureau of Indian Affairs

Bo Sweeney
Assistant Secretary

▲▼▲▼▲▼▲▼▲▼▲▼▲▼▲▼

ESTHER SHERMAN KEZENA

Last Will and Testament of Esther Sherman Kezena.

IN THE NAME OF GOD, AMEN.

I, Esther Sherman Kezena, being of sound mind do publish and declare this to be my last will and testament.

I bequeath to my father, Edgar Sherman all my real estate described as follows: N2 of SE/4 of Sec. 2 Twp. 94 Range 64 containing 80 acres and all located in Charles Mix County So. Dakota, said land now held in trust for me by the United States, known as allotment 1421-A.

2nd. I bequeath the remainder of my property consisting of household furnishings such as bed, stove, table, and sideboard to my husband, Jesse Kezena.

3rd. I give to my mother, Mrs. Susan Sherman, my infant son, Fred Clinton Kezena.

IN TESTIMONY WHEREOF, I have set my hand and seal this 27th day of January 1915, at Greenwood, So. Dakota, Charles Mix County.

Esther Sherman Kezena

Signed, sealed, published and declared this 27th day of Jan. 1915 by the said Esther Sherman Kezena in our presence, as for her last will and testament, and at her request and in her presence, and in the presence of each other we have hereunto subscribed our names as attesting witnesses.

Homer (Last Name Illegible)
Wm Henry Frederick

Department of The Interior,
Office of Indian Affairs, Washington,
AUG 26 1915

Indian Wills, 1911 – 1921 Book Three
Records of The Bureau of Indian Affairs

It is recommended that the within will be approved under the Act of June 25, 1910 (36 Stats. L., 855-6) as amended by Act of February 14, 1913 (37 Stats. L., 678).

Respectfully,

EB Meritt

Assistant Commissioner

Department of The Interior
Office of The Secretary   AUG 27 1915

The within will is hereby approved in accordance with the provisions of the Act of June 25, 1910 (36 Stats. L., 855-6) as amended by Act of February 14, 1913 (37 Stats. L., 678).

Bo Sweeney

Assistant Secretary

▲▼▲▼▲▼▲▼▲▼▲▼▲▼

WALKS WITH OWL

LAST WILL AND TESTAMENT

of

WALKS WITH OWL.

OFFICE OF INDIAN AFFAIRS
RECEIVED
SEP 19 1913
112520

OFFICE OF INDIAN AFFAIRS
RECEIVED
JUN 29 1915
72554

IN THE NAME OF GOD, Amen.

I, Walks With Owl, of Crow Creek Indian Reservation, Crow Creek, Buffalo County, South Dakota, being of sound mind, memory and understanding, do hereby make and publish this my last will and testament, hereby revoking and annulling all wills by me heretofore made, in manner and form following, that is to say:

FIRST, I direct that all my just debts and funeral expenses and the expenses of my last illness shall be paid by my executor hereinafter names as soon after my decease as shall be convenient.

SECOND, I give, devise and bequeath my own allotment of land within the Crow Creek Indian Reservation, Buffalo County, South Dakota, as follows: To my wife Hotanwin, the East Half of the Northeast quarter of Section 18, Township 107 North, Range 69 West, containing *80* acres; to my daughter Bessie Harrison, the Southwest quarter and the

97

South Half of the Northwest quarter of the Northeast quarter of Section 18, Township 107 North, Range 69 West, containing 60 acres; to my daughter Maggie Keble, the Northeast quarter of the Northwest quarter of Section 18, Township 107 North, Range 69 West, containing 40 acres; to my son Felix Walker, Lot 1 of Section 18, Township 107 North, Range 69 West, containing 37.12 acres; to my daughter Pearl Badger, Lot 2 of Section 18, Township 107 North. Range 69 West, containing 37.37 acres; to my son George Walker, the Southeast quarter of the Northwest quarter of Section 18, Township 107 North, Range 69 West, containing 40 acres; to my grandson Gilbert Walker, the North half of the Northwest quarter of the Northeast quarter of Section 18, Township 107 North, Range 69 West, containing 20 acres.

THIRD, I give and bequeath to my wife Hotanwin my set of harness. Of all funds and moneys due me or remaining on deposit to my credit after all of my just debts, funeral expenses and the expenses of my last illness shall have been paid, I give and bequeath one-third of all such funds, moneys and credits to my wife Hotanwin and the remaining two-thirds equally to Bessie Harrison, Maggie Keble, Felix Walker, Pearl Badger, George Walker, and Gilbert Walker, they being my children and grandchild, respectively.

AND LASTLY, I do hereby nominate, constitute and appoint the Reverend H. Burt, of Crow Creek, South Dakota, executor of this my last will and testament.

IN TESTIMONY WHEREOF, I have hereunto set my hand and seal to this my last will and testament at Crow Creek Agency Office, Crow Creek, South Dakota, this 21st day of July, A.D. 1913.

his

Walks With Owl [thumb print]

mark

Signed, sealed, published and declared by the said Walks With Owl in our presence as and for his last will and testament, and at his request and in his presence and in the presence of each other, we have hereunto subscribed our names as attesting witnesses thereto.

Homer J Bibb	Residence, Crow Creek, S.D.
Philip Bibb	Residence, Crow Creek, S.D.
John Bear	Residence, Crow Creek, S.D.

Department of The Interior,
Office of Indian Affairs, Washington,
AUG 10 1914
It is recommended that the within will be approved pursuant to the provisions of the Act of June 25, 1910 (36 Stats. L., 855-6) as amended by Act of February 14, 1913 (37 Stats. L., 678).

> Respectfully,
> *EB Meritt*
> Assistant Commissioner

Department of The Interior
Office of The Secretary   AUG 11 1914

The within will is hereby approved pursuant to the provisions of the Act of June 25, 1910 (36 Stats. L., 855-6) as amended by Act of February 14, 1913 (37 Stats. L., 678).

> *Bo Sweeney*
> Assistant Secretary

▲▼▲▼▲▼▲▼▲▼▲▼▲▼

CATHERINE WRIGHT

ACCIDENT DEPARTMENT

OFFICE OF INDIAN AFFAIRS
RECEIVED
MAR 23 1913
64599

Quapaw Indian Agency
Wyandotte, Okla.
Rec'd. *9/16/13*
No. *775*

Southern
Surety   Company

GENERAL OFFICES: NEW NATIONAL BANK OF COMMERCE BLDG

SAINT LOUIS, MISSOURI.

In the name of God amen:

I Catherine Wright of the city of Seneca, county of Newton and state of Missouri being now of usual health, strength of body and mind, but sensible to the uncertainty of life, and desiring to make disposition of my property and affairs, while in health and strength, do hereby make, publish and declare the following to be my last will and testament as to my real estate.

I do hereby bequeath to Martha Jane Wright, my Grand-Daughter the undivided half of what is known as the Caterine[sic] Wright Homestead. Situated in *N8 1/4 of SW1/4* in Section *19*. Township *29*, Range *25*

99

Wyandotte Reserve in the county of Ottawa, and the state of Oklahoma, consisting of 40 acres more or less. James Wright my son claims an undivided half in same.

In witness whereof I Catherine Wright have to this my last will and testament, consisting of one sheet of paper, subscribed my name this 19 day of May 1913.

her
Catherine x Wright
mark

The foregoing instrument, consisting of one page, was at the date thereof signed and declared by the said Catherine Wright to be her last will and testament, in the presence of us, who at her request and in her presence and in the presence of each other, have subscribed our names as witnesses thereto.

Louis Lofland – of Seneca Missouri
Caroline Lofland of Seneca Missouri

Department of The Interior,
Office of Indian Affairs, Washington,
Sept 6- 1913

It is recommended that the within will receive Departmental approval under the provisions of the Act of February 14, 1913 (37 Stats. L., 678).

CF Hawke
Second Assistant Commissioner

Department of The Interior
Office of The Secretary   SEP -6 1913

The within will approved pursuant to the provisions of the Act of February 14, 1913 (37 Stats. L., 678).

Assistant Secretary

▲▼▲▼▲▼▲▼▲▼▲▼▲▼

OFFICE OF INDIAN AFFAIRS
RECEIVED
JAN 13 1916
3616

TE BISH CO GWON

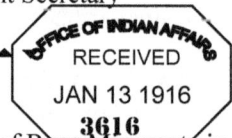

In the name of God, Amen: I, Te bish co gwon of Bena Minnesota in the county of Cass and state of Minnesta[sic], being of sound mind and memory, and considering the uncertainty of this frail and transitory life, do therefore make, ordain, publish and declare this to be my last will and testament.

Indian Wills, 1911 – 1921 Book Three
Records of The Bureau of Indian Affairs

FIRST, I order and direct that my executor hereinafter named, pay all my just debts and funeral expenses as soon after my decease as may be conveniently to do so.

SECOND, that after the payment of such funeral expenses an debts, I give and bequeath to my two daughters, Margaret Galbreath of Bena, Minnesota and Lousia Brown, of Ballclub, Minnesota, an equal share n all my personal estate, except as hereinafter described, including all my individual funds, which may be to my credit, and held in trust by the United States Government.

THIRD, I give and devise to my said two daughters, their heirs and assigns, all, Real Estate, allotted to me by the United States Govt. under provisions of the Act of Congress approved February 8th, 1887 (26 Stat. 794) and as provided for in the third scetion[sic] of the Act of January 14th, 1889 (25 State. 642), described as follows:

> Lots numbered three, four and five (3, 4 & 5) in
> Section twenty-nine (29), Township one hundred
> forty-five (145) in Range twenty-six (26).
> Allottment number 807.

Also all my interest in the following described real estate:

> Allottment of my deceased wife, Nah bun, #484:
> The north east quarter of the north west quarter,
> and the north west quarter of the northeast qr.
> of Section eight (8), Township one hundred
> forty-five (145) in Range twenty-six (26).

together with all the appurtences thereunto belonging, to have and to hold the same to them, the said Margaret Galbreath and Lousia Brown, their heirs and assigns, forever.

FOURTH, I give devise and bequeath to my son Nun sin e geshig, the sum of Five ($5.00) Dollars.

FIFTH AND LASTLY, I hereby constitute my son-inlaw[sic], George Galbreath to be executor of this, my last will and testament, hereby revoking all former wills by me made.

Indian Wills, 1911 – 1921 Book Three
Records of The Bureau of Indian Affairs

IN TESTIMONY WHEREOF, I have hereunto subscribed my hand and affixed my seal, this 3rd day of March in the year of our Lord 1915.

	his
Witnesses to mark:	*Tebish co gwon* [thumb print]
David W Smith	*mark*
Clement Smith	

The foregoing instrument was, on the day of the date thereof, signed, published and declared by the said testator to be his last will and testament in our presence, who, at his request, have subscribed our names thereto as witnesses, in his presence and in the presence of each other.

David W Smith	residing at	*Bena, Minn.*
WF Carmichael	residing at	*Bena Minn*
Clement Smith	residing at	*Bena, Minn*

I certify on honor that I have explained to the Indian who has executed this will, and am satisfied that he understood the nature and provisions of said will.

David W Smith
Interpreter.

Department of The Interior,
Office of Indian Affairs, Washington,
MAR 22 1916

It is recommended that the within will of Tebishcogwon be approved pursuant to the provisions of the Act of June 25, 1910 (36 Stats. L., 855-6) as amended by Act of February 14, 1913 (37 Stats. L., 678).

Respectfully,
EB Meritt
Assistant Commissioner

Department of The Interior
Office of The Secretary   MAR 23 1916

The within will of Tebishcogwon is hereby approved pursuant to the provisions of the Act of June 25, 1910 (36 Stats. L., 855-6) as amended by Act of February 14, 1913 (37 Stats. L., 678).

Bo Sweeney
Assistant Secretary

▲▼▲▼▲▼▲▼▲▼▲▼▲▼▲▼

KERSOME

OFFICE OF INDIAN AFFAIRS
RECEIVED
AUG 12 1913
98043 *Will*

OFFICE OF INDIAN AFFAIRS
RECEIVED
MAR 14 1916
27856

I, Kersome of Comanche County State of Oklahoma being now in good health, strength of body and mind, but sensible of the uncertainty of life and desiring to make disposition of my property and affairs while in health and strength, do hereby make and declare the following to be my last will and testament, hereby revoking and cancelling all other or former wills by me at any time made.

First. I direct the payment of all my just debts and funeral expenses.

Second. I give and devise to (Knox Taukawauard) Quittahui the following property my allottment, being the S.W.1/4 of Sec10 - 3W - 12W. Also any and all stock, money or other personal property of which I die possessed.

This will is made subject to the approval of the Secretary of the Interior.

In witness whereof I, Kersome, have to this my last will and testament, consisting of two sheets of paper, subscribed my name this 19th day of July 1913.

her thumb

Kersome [thumb print]

mark

Philip Burgess
  Interpreter

Subscribed by Kersome (testator) in the presence of each of us she undersigned and at the same time declared by her to us to be her last will and testament and we thereupon at the request of the testator Kersome in her presence, and in the presence of each other sign our names this nineteenth day of July 1913 at Mt. Scott Comanche County, State of Oklahoma.

Bettie V Burton,

Field Mation

  Mt. Scott, OK

Lily S Burton

Mount Scott Okla.

Department of The Interior,
Office of Indian Affairs, Washington,
AUG 25 1914

It is recommended that the within will be approved pursuant to the provisions of the Act of June 25, 1910 (36 Stats. L., 855-6) as amended by Act of February 14, 1913 (37 Stats. L., 678).

Respectfully,
EB Meritt
Assistant Commissioner

Department of The Interior
Office of The Secretary
AUG 27 1914

The within will is hereby approved pursuant to the provisions of the Act of June 25, 1910 (36 Stats. L., 855-6) as amended by Act of February 14, 1913 (37 Stats. L., 678).

Bo Sweeney
Assistant Secretary

Quapaw Indian Agency
Wyandotte, Okla.
Rec'd. JUN 15 1915
No.   8117

RED SUN QUAPAW

OFFICE OF INDIAN AFFAIRS
RECEIVED
SEP 25 1915
104073

I Red Sun Quapaw, Quapaw allottee No. 1898 of the Quapaw Agency, Ottawa Co, Okla. being in fairly good health, strength of body and good mind, but sensible of the uncertainty of life, and desiring to make disposition of my property, and affairs while in fair health and strength of body and mind, do hereby make, publish and declare the following to be my last will and testament hereby revoking and cancelling all other wills by me at any time made:

I hereby direct the payment of all my just debts and funeral expenses.

I give and devise to my daughter, Francis Quapaw Gokey, the following described real estate, to wit:- the SW1/4 of the NW1/4 and the NW1/4 of the SW1/4 of Section 4; and the SE1/4 of the NE1/4 and the NE1/4 of the SE1/4 of Section 5 all in Township 28, N.R. 24, E of I.M. Okla containing 160 acres

I give and devise to my husband, John Quapaw, the following described real estate to wit:- The NE1/4 of the NW1/4 of Section 3 Township 28 N, R.24 E of I.M. Okla and the NE1/4 of the NW1/4 of Section 34 Township 29 N R. 23 E, I.M. Okla containing 80 acres.

I give and devise to my grand children namely John Buffalo, Harve Buffalo, Clara May Buffalo, Hazel L Buffalo, Norah Buffalo and Willie Buffalo to be equally divided among these said children the following described real estate SE1/4 of SE1/4 Sec. 34 Township 29 N, R.23 E of I.M. containing 40 acres and all the remainder of my real estate inherited or otherwise.

In witness whereof I Red Sun Quapaw have to this my last will and testament consisting of two sheets of paper subscribed my name by thumb mark this 12th day of June 1915

her thumb mark
Red Sun Quapaw [thumb print]

*The name of Red Sun Quapaw was written by me at her request and in
her presence and thumb mark made by her in my presence*
Thank you
John W. Wyrick
Ray Thompson

*Subscribed by Red Sun Quapaw in the presence of each of us the
undersigned and at the same time declared by her to us to be her last will
and testament and we thereupon at the request of Red Sun Quapaw and
in her presence and in the presence of each other sign our names as
witnesses this 12th day of June 1915.*

John W Wyrick
Ray Thompson
Frank Kay

*I hereby certify that I have interpreted and translated the foregoing to
Red Sun Quapaw the testatrix at her request also to Frank Ray who drew
the will the entire contents and subject matter herein set forth and that
she had a full and thorough understanding of same.*

Mary Wyrick
Interpreter

Department of The Interior,
Office of Indian Affairs, Washington,
FEB 26 1916

It is recommended that the within will be approved according to the Act
of June 25, 1910 (36 Stats. L., 855-6) as amended by Act of February 14,
1913 (37 Stats. L., 678).

Respectfully,
EB Meritt
Assistant Commissioner

Department of The Interior
Office of The Secretary   FEB 28 1916

The within will is hereby approved according to the Act of June 25, 1910
(36 Stats. L., 855-6) as amended by Act of February 14, 1913 (37 Stats.
L., 678).

Indian Wills, 1911 – 1921 Book Three
Records of The Bureau of Indian Affairs

Bo Sweeney
Assistant Secretary

▲▼▲▼▲▼▲▼▲▼▲▼▲▼▲▼

GROS VENTRE HORSE

LAST WILL AND TESTAMENT

of

Gros Ventre Horse

IN THE NAME OF GOD, AMEN.

I, *Gros Ventre Horse* of *Crow Reservation, Mont,* being of sound mind, memory, and understanding, do hereby make and publish this my last will and testament, hereby revoking and annulling all wills by me heretofore made, in manner and form following, that is to say:

First; I direct that all my just debts and funeral expenses, and expenses of my last illness shall be paid by my executor hereinafter named as soon after my decease as convenient;

Second; I give, devise and bequeath to

My neice[sic]*, Goes-down-hill, wife of The Bread, the forty acre tract on which my home is located, with all buildings located therein. To Steven Driftwood, the forty acre tract adjoining me one above described and toward the hill. To Rides-the-sorrel-horse, my neice*[sic]*, to forty acre tract adjoining the first mentioned tract and lying toward the river. All the remainder of the land of which I may die possessed I give and bequeath to Susie Sweetmouth, Old Lodge Pole and Eli Blackhawk and Big Magpie, Goes-down-hill, Steven Driftwood and Rides-a-sorrel-horse, and Hazel Red-wolf, in equal shares, said land to be sold through though the regular channels to the highest bidder.*

All the rest and residue of my estate, both real, and personal and mixed, I give devise and bequeath to my heirs as determined by the Secretary of the Interior.

And lastly; I do hereby nominate, constitute and appoint *W.W. Scott, Superintendent, or his successor in Office* execut__ of this my last will and testament.

In Testimony Whereof, I have set my hand and seal to this, my last Will and Testament, at *Coyola*, Montana, this *22* day of *May*, in the year of our Lord one thousand nine hundred and *thirteen.*   His
                            Gros Ventre Horse [thumb print]
                                                        mark.

Signed, sealed, published and declared by said *Gros Ventre Horse* in our presence, as and for *his* last Will and Testament, and at *his* request and in our presence, and in the presence of each other, we have hereunto subscribed our names as attesting witnesses thereto.

Mary One Goose	of	*Coyola, Montana*
Dr. Edward (Illegible)	of	*Crow Agency, Mont*

Department of The Interior,
Office of Indian Affairs, Washington,
                    FEB 23 1916
It is recommended that the within will be approved according to the Act of June 25, 1910 (36 Stats. L., 855-6) as amended by Act of February 14, 1913 (37 Stats. L., 678).

                            Respectfully,
                            EB Meritt
                            Assistant Commissioner
Department of The Interior
Office of The Secretary   FEB 24 1916

The within will is hereby approved according to the Act of June 25, 1910 (36 Stats. L., 855-6) as amended by Act of February 14, 1913 (37 Stats. L., 678).

                            Bo Sweeney
                            Assistant Secretary

▲▼▲▼▲▼▲▼▲▼▲▼▲▼▲▼

HANNAH CARRIE WALKER GRANT

Last Will and Testament

of

Hannah Carrie Walker Grant

I, Hannah Carrie Walker Grant, of the Omaha Reservation, Thurston County, Nebraska, being of sound and disposing mind and memory, do hereby and by these presents make, publish and declare this instrument to be my last will and testament in manner and form following:

First

I am an Omaha Indian of the Omaha Tribe of Indians in Thurston County, Nebraska, and I am at present possessed of an allotment of forty acres of land on the Omaha Reservation, described as follows- the South east quarter of the Southwest quarter of Section 21, township 25 North of Range 9 East of the 6th P.M. Nebraska.

Second

I, give, devise and bequeath unto my two children. Mary Grant and Adam Grant, the Southeast quarter of the Southwest quarter of Section 21, Township 25 North of Range 9 East of the 6th P.M. Nebr. Share and share alike.

Third

I do hereby revoke any former will which I may have made.

Fourth

It is my desire that my mother take my children Mary and Adam Grant and care for them.

In witness whereof, I have here unto subscribed my name in Thurston County, Nebraska, this 9th day of July 1913, and I do hereby declare the above to be my last will and testament.
In presence of   *Her*
Edwin Walker   *Hannah Carrie Walker Grant* [thumb print]
B.A. Martindale   *mark*

The foregoing instrument was subscribed, published and declared by Hannah Carrie Walker Grant to be her last will and testament in our presence and in the presence of each of us and we at the same time as her request in her presence and in the presence of each other hereunto subscribed our names as attesting witnesses this 9th day of July, 1913.

> *Edwin Walker*
> *B.A. Martindale*

Department of The Interior,
Office of Indian Affairs, Washington,
JAN 29 1916
The within will is recommended for approval in accordance with the provisions of the Act of June 25, 1910 (36 Stats. L., 855-6) as amended by Act of February 14, 1913 (37 Stats. L., 678).

> Respectfully,
> *EB Meritt*
> Assistant Commissioner

Department of The Interior
Office of The Secretary   FEB -9 1916

The within will is hereby approved in accordance with the provisions of the Act of June 25, 1910 (36 Stats. L., 855-6) as amended by Act of February 14, 1913 (37 Stats. L., 678).

> *Bo Sweeney*
> Assistant Secretary

ALEXANDER L MARTIN

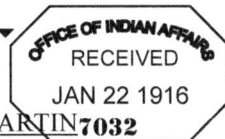

OFFICE OF INDIAN AFFAIRS
RECEIVED
NOV 20 1815
124427

OFFICE OF INDIAN AFFAIRS
RECEIVED
JAN 22 1916

THE LAST WILL OF ALEXANDER L MARTIN 7032

I, Alexander L Martin, Osage Allottee #1515 of Pawhuska, Oklahoma, do hereby make, publish and declare this my last Will and Testament in manner and form following.

<u>FIRST:</u> I give and devise unto my beloved wife, Minnie Martin, my homestead selection of land allotted me as a member of the Osage Tribe of Indians, described as follows, to-wit:

The Northeast Quarter of the Northeast Quarter and the South one-half of the Northeast quarter, and the Northeast Quarter of the Southeast Quarter of Section 8, Township 26, Range 11, in Osage County, Oklahoma.

SECOND: I give, bequeath and devise unto my beloved wife, Minnie Martin, all monies held in trust by the United States for me and segregated and placed to my credit under the Allotment Act: Also all my right, title and interest in and to the oil, gas and other minerals reserved to the Osage Tribe of Indians by the Allotment Act of June 28th, 1906, and all annuities accrued or to accrue by reason of my membership in the Osage Tribe of Indians.

THIRD: I give and bequeath to Mrs. Julia Patterson, Mrs. Aggie Ware, Mrs. Ellen McComb, Mrs. Rachael Blackburn, Lombard Martin and William Martin and Bertha Martin, each One Dollar ($1.00).

FOURTH: I nominate, constitute and appoint my wife, Minnie Martin, the executrix of this Will without bond.

FIFTH: I hereby revoke all former or other wills and Testamentary dispositions by me at anytime heretofore made.

IN TESTIMONY WHEREOF, I have hereto subscribed my name at Pawhuska, Oklahoma, this the 15th day of November, 1915.

Alex Martin

The foregoing instrument was subscribed, published and declared by Alexander L. Martin as and for his last Will and Testament, in our presence and in the presence of each of us, and we at the same time at his request, and in his presence, and in the presence of each other, hereto subscribed our names and residences as attesting witnesses, this the 15th day of November, 1915.

> *C.S. Macdonald*
> *Pawhuska, Okla.*
> *T.J. Leahy*
> *Pawhuska, Okla.*

Department of The Interior,
Office of Indian Affairs, Washington,
DEC 27 1915

It is recommended that the within will be approved in pursuance of the Act of April 18, 1912 (37 Stat. 86, 88).

Respectfully,

EB Meritt

12-JW-17   Assistant Commissioner

Department of The Interior
Office of The Secretary   DEC 27 1915

The within will is hereby approved in pursuance of the Act of April 18, 1912 (37 Stat. 86, 88).

Bo Sweeney

Assistant Secretary

▲▼▲▼▲▼▲▼▲▼▲▼▲

OFFICE OF INDIAN AFFAIRS
RECEIVED
NOV 4- 1915
118225

ME-HUN-KAH

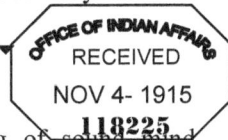

I, Me-hun-kah, Osage Allottee No. 621, being of sound mind, memory and understanding do make, publish and declare this instrument to be my last will and testament, to-wit:

1. I direct that my last sickness and funeral expenses be paid as soon as may be after my death.

2. I devise and bequeath unto my nearest relative, Joseph Mills, Osage Allottee No. 419, my homestead allotment and all of my trust fund, except $25.00 or other money belonging to my estate on deposit either at the Osage Agency or in the United States Treasury. I also give and bequeath to the said Joseph Mills all money or other personal property that I may inherit from the estate of my deceased son, William Shah-pah-nah-she, Osage Allottee No. 622. I also devise and bequeath to the said Joseph Mills all of my estate real, personal or mixed which I inherited from the estate of Helen Gibson, deceased Osage Allottee No. 231, being a one-fourth interest in said estate.

3. I devise my second selection of land, taken by me under the Allotment Act of June 28, 1906, into Carrie Shah-pah-nah-she, Osage Allottee No. 618.

4. I devise the remainder of my unsold surplus land taken by me under the aforesaid Allotment Act unto Christopher Shah-pah-nah-she,

unallotted child of Pah-se-to-pair, Osage Allottee No. 615.

5. Should I be found to be an heir of the estate of my deceased son, William Shah-pah-nah-she, I devise my inherited interest in the homestead allotment of my said son, William Shah-pah-nah-she, unto Lo-hah-me (Dora Little Bear), Osage Allottee No. 434.

6. Should I be found to be an heir of the estate of my deceased son, William Shah-pah-nah-she, I devise my inherited interest in the second selection allotted to my said son, William Shah-pah-nah-she unto Pah-se-to-pair, Osage Allottee No. 615.

7. Should I be found to be an heir of the estate of my deceased son, William Shah-pah-nah-she, I devise my inherited interest in the third selection allotted to my said son, William Shah-pah-nah-she unto Pierce St. John, Osage Allottee No. 623.

8. Should I be found to be an heir of the estate of my deceased son, William Shah-pah-nah-she, I devise my inherited interest in the remainder of surplus land allotted to my said son William Shah-pah-nah-she unto Anthony Mills, unallotted child of Joseph Mills, Osage Allottee No. 419. I also devise and bequeath the house in which I am now living in the Indian Village at Pawhuska, Oklahoma, unto the said Anthony Mills.

9. I devise and bequeath my house in the Indian Village in which Pah-sa-to-pah is now living unto Kathleen Shah-pah-nah-she unallotted child of said Pah-se-to-pah.

10. Should a child be born to my deceased son, William Shah-pah-nah-she and his wife Bertha Shah-pah-nah-she, I bequeath to said child the sum of $25.00 from my trust funds.

11. All the rest, residue and remainder of my estate, real, personal or mixed I devise and bequeath to the said Joseph Mills, Osage Allottee No. 419.

All of the above mentioned devises or restricted lands are made under and subject to the provision that said lands shall not be alienated or encumbered without the consent of the Secretary of the Interior.

In witness whereof, I, Me-hun-kah, have this *4th* day of September 1915 set my hand.

her

Me hun kah [thumb print]

I subscribed the name of Me-hun-kah   *mark*

at her request and witnessed her mark.

Arthur Bonnicastle

Signed, published and declared by Me hun-kah, Osage Allottee No. 621, as and for her last will and testament and attested by us as subscribing witnesses who signed our names hereto at the request of and in the presence of said testatrix and in the presence of each other.

Witnesses:

        Henry (Last Name Illegible)   *Pawhuska, Okla.*
        Walker Penn   *Pawhuska, Okla.*

Certificate of Interpreter.

I, the undersigned official interpreter of the Osage Agency at Pawhuska, Oklahoma, hereby certify that I interpreted the above and foregoing instrument truly and correctly from English into Osage and explained the same fully to Me-hun-kah and made her acquainted with the contents of the instrument and she thoroughly understands the same.

In testimony whereof, I have hereunto set my hand this 4th day of September, 1915.

        Arthur Bonnicastle
        Interpreter.

Department of The Interior,
Office of Indian Affairs, Washington,

It is recommended that the within will be approved in pursuance of the Act of April 18, 1912 (37 Stat. 86, 88).

        Respectfully,
        EB Meritt

1-SJC-3   Assistant Commissioner

Department of The Interior
Office of The Secretary   JAN 18 1916

Indian Wills, 1911 – 1921 Book Three
Records of The Bureau of Indian Affairs

The within will is hereby approved in pursuance of the Act of April 18, 1912 (37 Stat. 86, 88).

Bo Sweeney
Assistant Secretary

▲▼▲▼▲▼▲▼▲▼▲▼▲

AUGUSTUS FRONKIER

OFFICE OF INDIAN AFFAIRS
RECEIVED
MAY -6 1914
49471

LAST WILL OF AUGUSTUS FROMKIER[sie]
OSAGE ALLOTTEE #1258

I, Augustus Fronkier, Osage Allottee #1258, of Osage County, State of Oklahoma, being of sound mind, and realizing the uncertainty of life, do hereby make, declare and publish this, my last will and testament, hereby revoking any and all other wills or testaments heretofore made.

1st. It is my desire that out of my trust funds received from oil and gas royalties, the expenses of my last sickness and funeral expenses shall be paid.

2nd. I give and bequeath to each of my following relatives the sum of One Dollar, namely:

> Benjamin Fronkier,
> Phillip Fronker[sic],
> Laura Soligny.
> Simon Fronkier,
> Katherine Soldani,
> Josephine Soldani.

3rd. I give, bequeath and devise to my beloved wife, Jeannette Fronkier, all the residue of my property, personal, mixed and real estate of which I may die seized or possessed.

4th. It is my desire that Jeannette Fronkier be and I hereby appoint and constitute her the sole executrix of this my last will and testament, without bond.

IN WITNESS WHEREOF, I have hereunto set my hand at Pawhuska this 20th day of January, 1914.

Augustus Fronkier

114

The foregoing instrument was subscribed and published and delivered by Augustus Fronkier as and for his last will and testament in our presence and in the presence of each of us, and we, at the same time, at his request in his presence and in the presence of each other, hereto subscribe our names and residences as attesting witnesses at Pawhuska, Oklahoma, this 20th day of January, 1914.

Witnesses:

Victoria Isnard	Pawhuska, Oklahoma.
Chas S Macdonald	Pawhuska, Oklahoma.

Department of The Interior,
Office of Indian Affairs, Washington,

JUN 8 1914

It is recommended that the within will be approved pursuant to the provisions of the Act of June 25, 1910 (36 Stats. L., 855-6) as amended by Act of February 14, 1913 (37 Stats. L., 678).

Respectfully,
EB Meritt
Assistant Commissioner

Department of The Interior
Office of The Secretary

JUN 9 1914

The within will is approved pursuant to the provisions of the Act of June 25, 1910 (36 Stats. L., 855-6) as amended by Act of February 14, 1913 (37 Stats. L., 678).

(Signature Illegible)
Assistant Secretary

▲▼▲▼▲▼▲▼▲▼▲▼▲▼

DAHMANE WOOD BROWN

WILL OF DAHMANE WOOD BROWN

I, Dahmane Wood Brown of the Omaha Tribe of Indians and a resident of Thurston County, Nebraska, being of sound mind and memory, do hereby and by there presents make, publish and declare this will to be my last Will and Testament, hereby revoking any former will which I may have made.

115

Indian Wills, 1911 – 1921 Book Three
Records of The Bureau of Indian Affairs

First.

I give and bequeath and devise unto my husband John Brown my own allotment, the west one half of northwest quarter of section 36 township 25, N. R. 8 East of the 6th Principal Meridian and consisting of 80 acres.

Second.

I give and bequeath and devise unto my daughters, Mary Wood and Grace Wood my undivided interest in Henry Wood allotment, consisting of the southwest quarter of section 36 township 25, N. R. 9 East of the 6th Principal Meridian and consisting of a one fourth interest in the above described tract, to share equally.

Third.

I give and bequeath and devise unto my daughters Mary Wood and Grace Wood each one half interest in my undivided share of the George Peabody allotment, consisting of lots *3* and 4 the sounth[sic] one half of the northwest fractional quarter of section 3 township 24 N. R. 9 East of 6th Principal Meridian. Provided that my husband John Brown receives one third of the rental paid on said undivided share; upon the sale of the above undivided interest my husband John Brown is to receive the equivalent of a one third life interest on said undivided share.

Fourth.

I request that my minor daughter Grace Wood be adopted by Spafford Woodhull and his wife Dasabewe Cook Woodhull in accordance with the laws of the State of Nebraska.

Fifth.

I give devise and bequeath to my husband John Brown all personal property of which I may be possessed at the time of my death.

In witness whereof I have hereunto set my hand this first day of July, 1915, in the presence of: *her*

Dahmane Wood[thumb print]

Witnesses: *mark*

116

Indian Wills, 1911 – 1921 Book Three
Records of The Bureau of Indian Affairs

Parish Sannsoci
Spafford Woodhull

We, the undersigned do hereby certify that we have signed the above instrument as subscribing witnesses in the presence of each other and at his[sic] request and said instrument was explained to her (testator) in our presence and she understood the same and said testator did thereupon sign her name to same.

Parish Sannsoci
Spafford Woodhull

Signed to and sworn to before me this first day of July, 1915.

> *Axel Johnson*
> Superintendent.

(Note: No approval for above will given.)

▲▼▲▼▲▼▲▼▲▼▲▼▲▼▲▼

JACOB RIBS

Original
WILL

I, **Jacob Ribs** of Pine Ridge Agency, South Dakota, Allottee number **6479** do hereby make and declare this to be my last will and testament, in accordance with Section 2 of the Act of June 25, 1910, (36 stat. 855-858) and Act of February 14, 1913, (Public No. 381), hereby revoking all former wills made by me:

1. I hereby direct that as soon as possible after my decease, that all my debts, funeral and testamentary expenses be paid out of my personal estate.

2. I give and devise my allotment on the Pine Ridge Reservation, South Dakota, described as follows:

SE/4 of Sec. 12, T 36 N, R 45 W. 160 acres.

in the following manner:

all to my father, Ribs.

117

3. I give and bequeath all of my personal property of whatsoever nature and wheresoever situated unto

4. All the rest of my property, real or personal, now possessed or hereafter acquired, of whatsoever nature and wheresoever situated, I hereby give, devise and bequeath unto

my wife, Susie Ribs, two mares, issue harness and issue wagon.

The remainder of my property, consisting of three horses and seven head of cattle, to my father, Ribs.

In witness whereof I have hereunto set my hand this 24**th** day of **February** 191**5**.

Jacob Ribs

The above statement was, this **24th** day of **February** 191**5** signed and published by **Jacob Ribs** as **his** last will and testament, in the joint presence of the undersigned, the said **Jacob Ribs** then being of sound and vigorous mid and free from any constraint or compulsion; whereupon we, being without any interest in the matter other than friendship, and being well acquainted with **him** but not members of **his** family, immediately subscribed our names hereto in the presence of each other and of the said testator, for the purpose of attesting the said will, as **he** requested us to do.

	Post Office Address
H.E. Wright	**Pine Ridge, S. D.**
Joseph Red Sack	**Pine Ridge, S. D.**

Pine Ridge, South Dakota.
DEC 6 1915

I hereby certify that I have fully inquired into the mental competency of the Indian signing the above will; the circumstances attending the execution of the will; the influence that may have induced its execution, and the names of those entitled to share in the estate under the law of descent in South Dakota: reasons for the disposition of the property proposed by the will differing from disposition had the property descended by operation of law.

I respectfully forward this will with the recommendation that it be *dis*approved.

John R Brennan
Supt. & Spl. Disb. Agent.

Department of The Interior,
Office of Indian Affairs, Washington,

The within will is hereby recommended for approval in accordance with the provisions of the Act of June 25, 1910 (36 Stats. L., 855-6) as amended by Act of February 14, 1913 (37 Stats. L., 678).

Respectfully,

E B Meritt

Acting Assistant Commissioner

Department of The Interior

Office of The Secretary JAN 11 1917

The within will is hereby approved in accordance with the Act of June 25, 1910 (36 Stats. L., 855-6) as amended by Act of February 14, 1913 (37 Stats. L., 678).

Bo Sweeney

Assistant Secretary

▲ ▼ ▲ ▼ ▲ ▼ ▲ ▼ ▲ ▼ ▲ ▼ ▲ ▼

BLANCHE BLACK ROAD

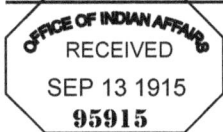

OFFICE OF INDIAN AFFAIRS
RECEIVED
SEP 13 1915
95915

Original
WILL

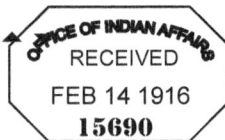

OFFICE OF INDIAN AFFAIRS
RECEIVED
FEB 14 1916
15690

   I, **Blanche Black Road** of Pine Ridge Agency, South Dakota, Allottee number **3275** do hereby make and declare this to be my last will and testament, in accordance with Section 2 of the Act of June 25, 1910, (36 stat. 855-858) and Act of February 14, 1913, (Public No. 381), hereby revoking all former wills made by me:

1. I hereby direct that as soon as possible after my decease, that all my debts, funeral and testamentary expenses be paid out of my personal estate.

2. I give and devise my allotment on the Pine Ridge Reservation, South Dakota, described as follows:

   E/2 of Sec. 25 T. 38 N., R. 48 W of the 6th P.M. in South Dakota containing 320 acres.

in the following manner:

To my daughter **Elizabeth Poor Elk** I bequeath the South one third 1/3 containing 106 2/3 acres.

To my daughter **Susie Whirlwing Bear** I bequeath the North 1/3 of the above described 320 acres containing 1/6 2/3 A.

To my grandchildren, being the children of my deceased son **Thos Rabbit**; **Silas Rabbit & Geo. Rabbit** I bequeath the balance.

3. I give and bequeath all of my personal property of whatsoever nature and wheresoever situated unto

My burial expenses to be paid from the benefit money on deposit, and $20,00[sic] to be paid to my brother Grant Short Bull for care while being sick at his home, bal. to be divided.

4. All the rest of my property, real or personal, now possessed or hereafter acquired, of whatsoever nature and wheresoever situated, I hereby give, devise and bequeath unto

To be divided evenly among my lawful heirs.

In witness whereof I have hereunto set my hand this **24th** day of **August, 1915.**   *her*
Witnesses to Signature by mark: *Blanche Black Road* [thumb print]
L L Smith   *mark*
Farmer, Oglala, S.D.
M R Eagle
Ass't Farmer, Oglala, S.D.

The above statement was, this **24th** day of **August 1915** signed and published by **Blanche Black Road** as **her** last will and testament, in the joint presence of the undersigned, the said **Blanche Black Road** then being of sound and vigorous mid and free from any constraint or compulsion; whereupon we, being without any interest in the matter other than friendship, and being well acquainted with **her** but not members of **her** family, immediately subscribed our names hereto in the presence of each other and of the said testator, for the purpose of attesting the said will, as **she** requested us to do. And that I, **L.L. Smith** at the testa**trixes** request have written **her** name in ink, and that **I** affixed **her** thumb-mark.

Post Office Address

L L Smith	**Farmer**	**Oglala, S. D.**
M R Eagle	Ass't "	**Oglala, S. D.**

Pine Ridge, South Dakota.
AUG 30 1915

I hereby certify that I have fully inquired into the mental competency of the Indian signing the above will; the circumstances attending the execution of the will; the influence that may have induced its execution, and the names of those entitled to share in the estate under the law of descent in South Dakota: reasons for the disposition of the property proposed by the will differing from disposition had the property descended by operation of law.

I respectfully forward this will with the recommendation that it be *dis*approved.

John R Brennan
Supt. & Spl. Disb. Agent.

Department of The Interior,
Office of Indian Affairs, Washington,
NOV 24 1915

It is recommended that the within will be approved pursuant to the provisions of the Act of June 25, 1910 (36 Stats. L., 855-6) as amended by Act of February 14, 1913 (37 Stats. L., 678).

Respectfully,
EB Meritt
Assistant Commissioner

Department of The Interior
Office of The Secretary
NOV 29 1915

The within will is approved pursuant to the provisions of the Act of June 25, 1910 (36 Stats. L., 855-6) as amended by Act of February 14, 1913 (37 Stats. L., 678).

Bo Sweeney
Assistant Secretary

▲▼▲▼▲▼▲▼▲▼▲▼▲▼▲

HOWASTEWIN

DEPARTMENT OF THE INTERIOR

UNITED STATES INDIAN SERVICE

OFFICE OF INDIAN AFFAIRS
RECEIVED
JUN -2 1915
61597

WILL OF HOWASTEWIN
121

Indian Wills, 1911 – 1921 Book Three
Records of The Bureau of Indian Affairs

IN THE NAME OF GOD AMEN:

I, Howastewin of the state of South Dakota, county of Charles Mix, being of sound and disposing mind and memory but being uncertain of life, and certain of the approach of death, and desiring to dispose of all my worldly possessions while I still have the power to do so, do make and declare this to be my last will and testament hereby revoking and annulling any and all wills hereto fore made by me.

1. I give and devise unto my daughter, Mary Doherty, (40 acres) forty acres of land of my original allotment described as follows SE1/4 of SE1/4 of section 36 T. 97 R. 66 west of the 5th P.M. Charles Mix County, So. Dak.

2. I give and devise unto my daughter, Mary Doherty, all my inherited interest in the estate of my deceased husband, Tasunkewaste, allotment #886 and described as the N 1/2 of SE 1/4 and the S 1/2 of the NE 1/4 of section 20, T. 96, R. 65 west of the 5th P.M. Charles Mix county, So. Dak.

3. I give and devise unto my daughter, Ada Kiyukan, (40 acres) forty acres of my original allotment, described as follows: SW 1/4 of SE 1/4 of section 36, T. 97, R. 66 west of the 5th P.M., Charles Mix county, So. Dak.

4. It is my desire that all the rest of my property, both real and personal, after the payment of the expenses of my last sickness and my funeral expenses, shall go to my daughter, Mary Doherty.

IN TESTIMONY WHERE, I HAVE SET MY HAND AND SEAL THIS THE 17TH, DAY OF MAY, IN THE YEAR OF OUR LORD 1915, AT LAKE ANDES, CHARLES MIX COUNTY, SOUTH DAKOTA.

HER

WITNESSES: HOWASTEWIN
Charles Moneke   MARK.
Anna Moneke
J Gassneau police

Signed, sealed, published and declared this 17th, day of May, 1915, by the said Howastewin in our presence, as and for her last will and testament, and at her request, and in her presence, and in the presence of each other we have hereunto subscribed our names as attesting witnesses.

N. Conner

J Gassneau

Department of The Interior,
Office of Indian Affairs, Washington,
JAN 27 1916
It is recommended that the within will of Howastewin be approved pursuant to the provisions of the Act of June 25, 1910 (36 Stats. L., 855-6) as amended by Act of February 14, 1913 (37 Stats. L., 678).

Respectfully,

EB Meritt

Assistant Commissioner

Department of The Interior
Office of The Secretary
JAN 28 1916
The within will of Howastewin is hereby approved pursuant to the provisions of the Act of June 25, 1910 (36 Stats. L., 855-6) as amended by Act of February 14, 1913 (37 Stats. L., 678).

Bo Sweeney

Assistant Secretary

▲▼▲▼▲▼▲▼▲▼▲▼▲▼

LUKE WHITE

Last Will and Testament of Luke White

I, Luke White, of the Omaha Reservation, in the County of Thurston, State of Nebraska, being of sound mind and memory, but realizing the uncertainties of life, do hereby make, ordain, publish, and declare this to be my Last Will and Testament.

1st. I desire that my wife, Ca-sa-we White, shall have the use of my allotment consisting of the North 1/2 and the SE1/4 of the NW1/4, Sec 23, Tp 25 N, R9E, 6th P.M. in Neb and the NE1/4 of the NE1/4 of Sec 20, Tp25, R7 same consisting of all reastate[sic] thereon so long as she may live.

Upon the death of my Ca-sa-we White, I desire that my allotment be divided as follows:

1st. I give, devise and bequeath to my step daughter, Ne da we Walker, who has cared for me as if I had been her own father, the North one half of the NW1/4 of Sec 23, Tp 25N, R9E of 6th PM in Neb and containing according to the Government survey eighty acres.

2nd. I give, devise, and bequeath to my grand daughter, Susie Walker, the SE1/4 of the NW1/4 of Sec 23, Tp 25, N, R9E of 6th PM in Neb and containing according to the Govt Survey forty acres.

3rd. I give, devise, and bequeath to my grand daughter, Daisy Walker, the NE1/4 of the NE1/4 of Sec. 20, Tp 25 N, Range 7E of 6th PM in Neb and containing according to the Govt Survey forty acres.

This Will is drawn subject to the conditions that no sale or conveyance by the devisees, their heirs, administrations, executors, or legal representatives, until the last one of them shall have attained majority, shall be valid unless approved by the Secretary of the Interior

Luke White [thumb print] *his mark*

This Instrument was on the 13th day of March 1912 signed, published and declared by the said testator Luke White to be his last Will and testament and we in the presence of each other and in his presence and at his request have subscribed our names hereto and are also witnesses to the thumb mark of the said testator.

> *Elva Walker*
> *Levi Levering*
> *Albert H Kinale*

Department of The Interior,
Office of Indian Affairs, Washington,
FEB 17 1916

It is recommended that the within will be approved pursuant to the provisions of the Act of June 25, 1910 (36 Stats. L., 855-6) as amended by Act of February 14, 1913 (37 Stats. L., 678).

> Respectfully,
> *EB Meritt*
> Assistant Commissioner

Indian Wills, 1911 – 1921 Book Three
Records of The Bureau of Indian Affairs

Department of The Interior
Office of The Secretary JAN 14 1921

The within will is hereby approved according to the provisions of the Act of June 25, 1910 (36 Stats. L., 855-6) as amended by Act of February 14, 1913 (37 Stats. L., 678).

Bo Sweeney
Assistant Secretary

▲▼▲▼▲▼▲▼▲▼▲▼▲▼

COAL OF FIRE

Original
WILL

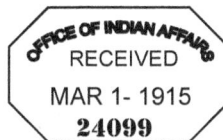

OFFICE OF INDIAN AFFAIRS
RECEIVED
MAR 1- 1915
24099

    I, **Coal of Fire** of Pine Ridge Agency, South Dakota, Allottee number **1829** do hereby make and declare this to be my last will and testament, in accordance with Section 2 of the Act of June 25, 1910, (36 stat. 855-858) and Act of February 14, 1913, (Public No. 381), hereby revoking all former wills made by me:

1. I hereby direct that as soon as possible after my decease, that all my debts, funeral and testamentary expenses be paid out of my personal estate.

2. I give and devise my allotment on the Pine Ridge Reservation, South Dakota, described as follows:

    the N/2 of Sec. 14 in Twp. 41 N. of Range 39 west of the Sixth Principal Meridian, South Dakota, containing 320 acres.

in the following manner:

    To my husband, Brown Eyes: the NE/4 of Sec. 14 in Twp. 41 N. of Range 39 west of the 6th P.M.
    To my step-daughter, Susie White Eyes: the NW/4 of Sec. 14 in Twp. 41 N. of Range 39 west of the 6th P.M.

3. I give and bequeath all of my personal property of whatsoever nature and wheresoever situated unto

to my husband, Brown Eyes.

4. All the rest of my property, real ~~or personal~~, now possessed or hereafter acquired, of whatsoever nature and wheresoever situated, I hereby give, devise and bequeath unto

to my husband, Brown Eyes, and my step-daughter, Susie White Eyes, in equal shares.

In witness whereof I have hereunto set my hand this **18th** day of **February** 1915.
                                                    her
                                        mark [thumb print]
                              Coal of Fire

The above statement was, this **18th** day of **February** 1915 signed and published by **Coal of Fire** as **her** last will and testament, in the joint presence of the undersigned, the said **Coal of Fire** then being of sound and vigorous mid and free from any constraint or compulsion; whereupon we, being without any interest in the matter other than friendship, and being well acquainted with **her** but not members of **her** family, immediately subscribed our names hereto in the presence of each other and of the said testator, for the purpose of attesting the said will, as **she** requested us to do., **her name being signed by George A. Trotter, one of the witnesses, at her request.**

	Post Office Address
George A Trotter	**Kyle, South Dakota.**
Peter Chiefeagle	**Kyle, South Dakota.**

Pine Ridge, South Dakota.
FEB 25 1915

I hereby certify that I have fully inquired into the mental competency of the Indian signing the above will; the circumstances attending the execution of the will; the influence that may have induced its execution, and the names of those entitled to share in the estate under the law of descent in South Dakota: reasons for the disposition of the property proposed by the will differing from disposition had the property descended by operation of law.

I respectfully forward this will with the recommendation that it be …..approved.

                              John R Brennan
                        Supt. & Spl. Disb. Agent.

Indian Wills, 1911 – 1921 Book Three
Records of The Bureau of Indian Affairs

Department of The Interior,
Office of Indian Affairs, Washington,
MAR 18 1916

It is recommended that the within will be approved in accordance with the Act of June 25, 1910 (36 Stats. L., 855-6) as amended by Act of February 14, 1913 (37 Stats. L., 678).

> Respectfully,
> *EB Meritt*
> Assistant Commissioner

Department of The Interior
Office of The Secretary MAR 28 1916

The accompanying will is hereby approved under the Act of June 25, 1910 (36 Stats. L., 855-6) as amended by Act of February 14, 1913 (37 Stats. L., 678).

> *Bo Sweeney*
> Assistant Secretary

▲▼▲▼▲▼▲▼▲▼▲▼▲▼

OFFICE OF INDIAN AFFAIRS
RECEIVED
APR 18 1916
36531

HENRY TAYOU

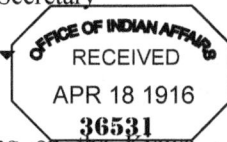

    I, Henry Tayou, Comanche Indian, residing on the Kiowa, Comanche and Apache Reservation, Caddo County, Oklahoma, being of sound and disposing mind, do make and publish this my last will and testament:

First:-
    I give and bequeath to my older sister *Wed yah vaud* one dollar.

Second:-
    I direct that all my funeral expenses be paid, from funds now belonging to me and held for my benefit at the Indian Agency in Anadarko, Okla.

Third:-
    I direct that one horse and a buggy belonging to me be given to my cousin, Ate woff take van, Comanche, No. 53 1/2.

Fourth:-
    I direct that all money remaining to my credit at the Agency in Anadarko, Okla. and also the allotment made to me, being No. 877 and

consisting of the following described land:-

The North West quarter of section thirty two in Township five North of Range Eleven West of the Indian Meridian in Oklahoma.
Containing one hundred and sixty Acres.
This allotment being recorded in Volume 82 Page 373.

I direct that this money and the above described land be divided equally between my Uncle Pake wo hap it, Comanche, #542 and my cousin, Ate woof take van, Comanche, No 53 1/2

Subscribed by me this twenty third day of September, 1915   *His*
                                                                Thumb
                     Henry Tayou [thumb print]   *mark*

Subscribed by Henry Ta you in the presence of each of us, the undersigned, and at the same time declared by him to us to be his last will and testament, and we, therupon[sic], at his request of said Henry Ta you, in his presence and in the presence of each other, sign our names as witnesses this 23 day of Semtember[sic], 1915

            Owen F Thompson   Post Office Address, Apache Okla.
            W. W. Carithers   Post Office Address, Apache Okla.

Department of The Interior,
Office of Indian Affairs, Washington,
APR 13 1916

It is recommended that the within will be approved according to the Act of June 25, 1910 (36 Stats. L., 855-6) as amended by Act of February 14, 1913 (37 Stats. L., 678).

                                      Respectfully,
                                      EB Meritt
                                      Assistant Commissioner

Department of The Interior
Office of The Secretary APR 21 1916

The within will is hereby approved according to the Act of June 25, 1910 (36 Stats. L., 855-6) as amended by Act of February 14, 1913 (37 Stats. L., 678).

Bo Sweeney
Assistant Secretary

▲▼▲▼▲▼▲▼▲▼▲

IDA MORRISON or BONE NECKLACE

WILL.

OFFICE OF INDIAN AFFAIRS
▲▼
RECEIVED
SEP -3 1915
95913

OFFICE OF INDIAN AFFAIRS
RECEIVED
APR 25 1916
44957

I, Ida Morrison or Bone Necklace of Pine Ridge Agency, South Dakota, Allottee number 4530, do hereby make and declare this to be my last will and testament, in accordance with Section 2 of the Act of June 25, 1910, (36 stat. 855-858) and Act of February 14, 1913, (Public No. 381), hereby revoking all former wills made by me:

1.

I hereby direct that as soon as possible after my decease, that all my debts, funeral and testamentary expenses be paid out of my personal estate.

2.

I give and devise my allotment on the Pine Ridge Reservation, South Dakota, described as follows: *West half of Section 32; T 27, north of range 26, west of the 6 P.M. Bennett Co, South Dakota;*

in the following manner:

The north 1/4 to my daughter, Mrs. Elizabeth Marshall

The south 1/4 to be sold and divided among my children.

3.

I give and bequeath all of my personal property of whatsoever nature and wheresoever situated unto *Mrs. Julia Bell Bear, one wagon and harness; to the person providing my coffin, one white horse;*

4.

129

All the rest of my property, real or personal, now possessed or hereafter acquired, of whatsoever nature and wheresoever situated, I hereby give, devise and bequeath unto *my children or heirs*

In witness whereof I have hereunto set my hand this *12* day of August, 1915.   *her*

Ida Morrison, Bone Necklace [thumb print]
                                                                                    mark

Witness to Mark.

    Sam Lessert
    H. M Robertson

The above statement was, this *12* day of August, 1915, signed and published by Ida Morrison as her last will and testament, in the joint presence of the undersigned, the said Ida Morrison then being of sound and vigorous mid and free from any constraint or compulsion; whereupon we, being without any interest in the matter other than friendship, and being well acquainted with her but not members of her family, immediately subscribed our names hereto in the presence of each other and of the said testator, for the purpose of attesting the said will, as she requested us to do, and that I *H.M. Robertson* at the testator's request, have written her name in ink and that I affixed her thumb-mark.

Witnesses names.	Addresses
Sam Lessert	*Martin, S. Dak.*
H M Robertson	*Martin, S Dak..*

State of South Dakota   )
County of Bennett   ) ss   Ida Morrison, (Bone Necklace, first being duly sworn, deposes and says that she has made the above disposition of her property for the reasons that she believes herself to be near the point of death and wishing that her children be given the benefit of her property as she has designated and that they should not be troubled in the use of said property by any obligation to pay *her* funeral expenses, or any other debts which she may leave after her death; *that she wills to Mrs. Joseph Marshal because Mrs. Joseph Marshal has supported her for several years.*   Her

        Ida Morrison Bone Necklace[thumb print]
Witnesses to Mark.   mark.
    Sam Lessert

H M Robertson

Subscribed and sworn to before me this *12th* day of August, 1915.

My Commission expires Feb. 12th., 191*8*   *Hastings M Robertson*
Notary Public

Pine Ridge, South Dakota.

AUG 30 1915

I hereby certify that I have fully inquired into the mental competency of the Indian signing the above will; the circumstances attending the execution of the will; the influence that may have induced its execution, and the names of those entitled to share in the estate under the law of descent in South Dakota: reasons for the disposition of the property disposed by the will differing from disposition had the property descended.

I respectfully forward this will with the recommendation that it be *dis* approved.

John R Brennan
Supt. & Spl. Disb. Agent.

Department of The Interior,
Office of Indian Affairs, Washington,
SEP 30 1915

It is recommended that the within will be approved according to the Act of June 25, 1910 (36 Stats. L., 855-6) as amended by Act of February 14, 1913 (37 Stats. L., 678).

Respectfully,
EB Meritt
Assistant Commissioner

Department of The Interior
Office of The Secretary OCT -1 1915

The within will is hereby approved according to the Act of June 25, 1910 (36 Stats. L., 855-6) as amended by Act of February 14, 1913 (37 Stats. L., 678).

Bo Sweeney
Assistant Secretary

▲▼▲▼▲▼▲▼▲▼▲▼▲▼▲▼

EUNICE IYUDUZA or ZIMMERMAN

Last Will of Eunice Iyuduza or Zimmerman.

IN THE NAME OF GOD, AMEN.

I, Eunice Iyuduza or Zimmerman, of the State of South Dakota, county of Charles Mix, being of sound and disposing mind and memory, but being uncertain of life and certain of the approach of death, and desiring to dispose of all my worldly possessions while I still have the power to do so, do make and declare this to be my last will and testament hereby revoking and annulling any and all wills heretofore made by me.

1. I direct that that portion of my land located on the Yankton Reservation, Charles Mix County South Dakota, described as the N1 of the NW/4 Section 12, Township 94 Range 62, be sold and from the proceeds derived from this sale I bequeath the sum of $1000. to the Presbyterian Church of Greenwood, South Dakota; I also bequeath from the money derived from the sale of this land the sum of $1000.00 each to my cousin, John Omaha, and my brother, Peter Necklace; and whatever balance remains from the proceeds of the sale of the above described land I bequeath equally to my cousin Sarah Kealear and my nieces Agnes Standingbull and Emma Standinbull[sic] Fielder, the three last mentioned parties to share alike.

2. I bequeath to my brother-in-law, Moses Standingbull the SW/4 of the SW/4 of Section 14, Township 94, Range 62.

3. I bequeath to my sister in law, Margaret Necklace, the NW/4 of the NE/4 Section 22, Township 94 Range 62.

4. I bequeath to my niece, Emma Standingbull Fielder the NE/4 of the NE/4 Section 22 Township 94 Range 62.

5. I bequeath to my nephew, Samuel Baker, the NW/4 of the NW/4 Section 23 Township 94, Range 62.

6. I bequeath to my niece, Emma Standingbull Fielder, the house consisting of two rooms owned by me and situated on the agency reserve at Greenwood, South Dakota.

7.   I bequeath to Minnie Kealear Hopkins 5 head of horses consisting of one mare and four colts, now in the possession of John Graham on Corn Creek, Pine Ridge Reservation South Dakota.

8.   I bequeath to my brother, Peter Necklace, the 40 acres of land inherited from my son Thomas Iyuduza described as the NE/4 of the NE/4 Section 9, Township 93, Range 63 (Law Heirship 84380-14 E S M) and any money that may remain to my credit in the hands of the superintendent of the Yankton Indian Agency after my just debts and funeral expenses have been paid and a monument erected on my grave.

9.   I bequeath to my lawful heirs all properties that may now belong to me or at any later period be awarded to me from any estates to which I may be an heir either on this reservation or any other reservation.

IN TESTIMONY WHEREOF, I have set my hand and seal this 27th of April, 1915, at Greenwood, Charles Mix County, South Dakota.

                                                                              her
Interpreter   Eunice Iyuduza or Zimmerman [thumb print]
John P Williamson

Signed, SEALED[sic], PUBLISHED[sic] and declared on the 27th day of April, 1915, by the said Eunice Iyuduza or Zimmerman, in our presence, as and for her last will and testament, and at her request, and in her presence, and in the presence of each other, we have here unto subscribed our names as attesting witnesses.

                                             G W Williamson
                                             John Omaha

Department of The Interior,
Office of Indian Affairs, Washington,
                              MAR 31 1916

It is recommended that the within will be under the provisions of the Act of June 25, 1910 (36 Stats. L., 855-6) as amended by Act of February 14, 1913 (37 Stats. L., 678).

                                             Respectfully,
                                             EB Meritt
                                             Assistant Commissioner

Department of The Interior
Office of The Secretary   APR 25 1916

The within will is hereby approved under the provisions of the Act of June 25, 1910 (36 Stats. L., 855-6) as amended by Act of February 14, 1913 (37 Stats. L., 678).

Bo Sweeney
Assistant Secretary

▲▼▲▼▲▼▲▼▲▼▲▼▲▼

WILLIAM THOMAS SCHUYLER

Last Will of William Thomas Schuyler Oneida allottee No. 945.

DEPARTMENT OF THE INTERIOR

UNITED STATES INDIAN SERVICE

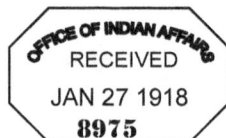

Oneida, Wisconsin, January 25, 1916

OFFICE OF INDIAN AFFAIRS
RECEIVED
JAN 27 1918
8975

I, William Thomas Schuyler, of the Town of Oneida, County of Outagamie, and state of Wisconsin, a widower, do make this my last Will and Testament:

I give and bequeath to my daughter, Rose S. King, and to my five sons, Anderson Schuyler, James Schuyler, George Schuyler, Thomas Schuyler and William T. Schuyler, in equal shares, all real and personal property of which I may die possessed and especially the land which I now hold under the trust patent No. 945, consisting of the North West Quarter of the South East Quarter of Section 24, T. 23 N. R 18 R. of the 4th P.M. Wisconsin, containing forty acres.

I make no provision for my daughter, Electa S. Metoxen, and for my wife's son, known as Wilson Schuyler, who are of age and each received an allotment of land.

IN WITNESS WHEREOF, I have signed and sealed this instrument, and published and declared the same as and for my last will, at Oneida, Wisconsin, this 25th day of January, 1916.

Witnesses to mark.
Samuel A Bell
Frank Whiteter

William Thomas Schuyler [thumb print]
his mark

At Oneida, Wisconsin, on this 25th day of January, 1916, the above named William Thomas Schuyler signed and sealed this instrument, and published and declared the same as and for his last will, and we, at his request, and in his presence, and in the presence of each other, have hereunto subscribed our names as witnesses.

JC Hart   Supt
Samuel A Bell

Department of The Interior,
Office of Indian Affairs, Washington,
APR 22 1916

The within will is recommended for approval in accordance with the Act of June 25, 1910 (36 Stats. L., 855-6) as amended by Act of February 14, 1913 (37 Stats. L., 678).

Respectfully,
EB Meritt
Assistant Commissioner

Department of The Interior
Office of The Secretary   APR 24 1916

The within will is approved in accordance with the Act of June 25, 1910 (36 Stats. L., 855-6) as amended by Act of February 14, 1913 (37 Stats. L., 678).

Bo Sweeney
Assistant Secretary

▲▼▲▼▲▼▲▼▲▼▲▼▲▼▲▼

FRANK BUCK or SANSWAY BEARGREASE

LAST WILL AND TESTAMENT.

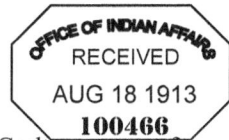

OFFICE OF INDIAN AFFAIRS
RECEIVED
AUG 18 1913
100466

I, Frank Buck, of Cloquet, in the county of Carlton, state of Minnesota, being of sound mind and memory, and considering the uncertainties of life, do therefore make, publish and declare this to be my last will and testament.

First, I order and direct that my debts and funeral expenses shall be paid as soon after my decease as conveniently may be, said debts and expenses to be paid from my individual bank account.

Second, I give and bequeath to Daniel Drumbeater, son of my niece Sophia Drumbeater, one hundred ($100.00) dollars in cash, same to be paid from my individual bank account.

Third, I give and bequeath to my wife, Elizabeth Buck, one-half (1/2) of all my real estate, consisting of original and inherited Indian lands, except my homestead of forty acres, (2) one-half (1/2) of all moneys in bank, after my debts and funeral expenses have been paid and the one hundred ($100.00) dollars cash bequeathed to Daniel Drumbeater has been deducted, (3) all stock and household goods and furniture, (4) and the free and unrestricted use of my homestead during her life.

Fourth, I give and bequeath to my daughter, Leona Buck, one-half (1/2) of all my real estate, consisting of original and inherited Indian lands, except my homestead of forty acres, (2) one-half (1/2) of all moneys in bank, after my debts and funeral expenses have been paid and the one hundred ($100.00) dollars cash bequeathed to Daniel Drumbeater has been deducted, (3) and upon the death of my wife, Elizabeth Buck, the free and unencumbered possession of my homestead heretofore mentioned.

Fifth, Any and all former wills by me made are hereby revoked.

IN TETIMONY WHEREOF, I have hereunto subscribed my name and affixed my seal this 26th day of March, 1913.

Frank Buck

This instrument was, on the date thereof signed, published, and declared by the said testator, Frank Buck, to be his last will and testament in our presence, who at his request have subscribed our names thereto as witnesses in his presence and in the presence of each other.

John Bassett	residing at	*Cloquet Minn*
Sam Edwards	residing at	*Cloquet Minn*

Department of The Interior,
Office of Indian Affairs, Washington,
APR -1 1916

The within will of Frank Buck or Sansway Beargrease is recommended for approval in accordance with the Act of June 25, 1910 (36 Stats. L., 855-6) as amended by Act of February 14, 1913 (37 Stats. L., 678), in so far as it applies to lands within the jurisdiction of the Department

Cate Sells
Commissioner

Department of The Interior
Office of The Secretary APR 24 1916

The within will of Frank Buck or Sansway Beargrease is recommended for approval in accordance with the Act of June 25, 1910 (36 Stats. L., 855-6) as amended by Act of February 14, 1913 (37 Stats. L., 678), in so far as it applies to lands within the jurisdiction of the Department

Franklin K Payne
Secretary

The White House,
11 April, 1916

Approved:

Woodrow Wilson

▲▼▲▼▲▼▲▼▲▼▲▼▲▼▲▼

CHARLES EDMOND FULLER

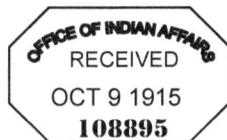

LAST WILL AND TESTAMENT

OF

```
OFFICE OF INDIAN AFFAIRS
RECEIVED
OCT 9 1915
108895
```

CHARLES FULLER

I, Charles Fuller of Osage County, Oklahoma, being of sound mind and disposing memory, realizing the uncertainty of life and the certainty of death, do hereby make, publish and declare this my last will and testament, hereby revoking and annulling all other wills heretofore by me made.

ITEM I.

Out of my estate I direct that all of my just debts and funeral expenses shall be first paid, and that a suitable monument, costing not to exceed TWO HUNDRED AND FIFTY ($250.00) Dollars shall be erected at my grave. In case, however, my remains should be placed in a Mausoleum then no monument need be erected.

ITEM II.

I will, devise and bequeath my homestead consisting of One Hundred Sixty (160) acres, in Osage County, Oklahoma, and being the East one-half of the Northeast quarter of Section Twenty-five (25), Township Twenty-nine (29) Range Five (5) East all in Osage County, Oklahoma, to my beloved son, Charles Edmond Fuller. Provided, however, that if my said son should die unmarried and without issue prior to the death of my wife, then I will and bequeath said property to my wife, Sarah Edith Fuller.

ITEM III.

I will, devise and bequeath the East one-half of Section Fourteen (14), Township Twenty-nine (29) Range Five (5) East and the Southeast quarter of Section Thirty-four (34), Township Twenty-seven (27), Range Ten (10) east, all in Osage County, Oklahoma, in trust to my executor to be disposed of as follows:

My executor, after consulting with my wife and my son as to the best manner and time of selling and disposing of said real estate, shall after taking a proper and due length of time in order to get the best price obtainable for said land, sell and dispose of the same, either in bulk or in parcels, for the highest price and upon the best terms obtainable, and may take as part payment for the same, notes well and properly secured by first real estate mortgages, provided that the rate of interest on the notes secured by said mortgage shall be the highest obtainable under the circumstances, and my said executor shall invest and keep invested the proceeds of the sale of said land in good first real estate mortgages and shall pay the proceeds of said investment to my said wife Sarah Edith Fuller during her natural life for the support of herself and for the support and education of my son, Charles Edmond Fuller during his minority. In case my said son should die unmarried and without issue prior to the death of my said wife, then the proceeds of the sale of said land shall be turned over and become the absolute property of my said wife. In case my wife should die before my son becomes of majority then the proceeds of the sale of said land shall continue to be invested as hereinbefore provided , but the income thereof shall be applied to the support and education of my said son until he becomes of age, and when my said son Charles Edmond Fuller attains his majority, in case my said wife should die prior to his majority, or at the time of the death of my said wife in case she should live until after my said son reaches his majority, then the entire amount of the proceeds of the sale of said land, together with any increase thereto by reason of the investment of the same, shall become the absolute property of my said son, Charles Edmond Fuller. In case my said son, Charles Edmond Fuller, should die unmarried and without issue after the death of my wife, and before he reaches his majority, then one-fourth of the proceeds of the sale of said land, together with one-fourth of the amount of any unused income derived from the investment of the same, shall become the absolute property of Mickie Crouse, the son of my sister, Isabell Fuller Crouse, and one-fourth of the proceeds of the sale of said land, together with one-fourth of the amount of any unused income derived from the investment of the same, shall become the absolute property of Andrew Stephen Fuller, and one-fourth of the proceeds of the sale of said land, together with one-fourth of the amount of any unused income derived from the investment of the same, shall become the absolute property of Ima Field Otey, and one-fourth of the proceeds of the sale of said land, together with one-fourth of the amount of any unused income derived from the investment of the same, shall become the absolute property of Samuel Hayes Fuller. My executor is further directed that in case all the income derived from the proceeds of the sale of the above mentioned land shall not be necessary for the support of my said wife as herein provided, or for the support and education of my son, then the unused income shall be reinvested on the same conditions as the original proceeds of the sale of said land and shall become a part of the principal.

ITEM IV.

I will, devise and bequeath the Ten (10) acres of land which I now own in the State of Florida, being known and designated as Lots Five (5) and Six (6) and located near Palm Beach, Florida, and about sic (6) miles from Delray, Florida, to my son Charles Edmond Fuller; Provided, however, that the taxes on the same shall be paid out of the income derived from the proceeds of the sale of land as provided in Item Three (3) hereof.

ITEM V.

I further will and direct that all of my watches, rings, jewelry, riding saddles and riding bridles shall be by my executor kept for my son Charles Edmond Fuller until he reaches the age of 21 years, and shall then be turned over to him and become his absolute property.

ITEM VI.

I will, devise and bequeath all the rest, residue and remainder of my personal property of whatsoever kind and wheresoever situated, to my wife Sarah Edith Fuller, to be hers absolutely and forever.

ITEM VII.

In the payment of my debts I direct that the proceeds of the sale of my personal property shall be first applied to the payment of the same, and that the trust fund created in Item Three (3) hereof shall be the last to be taken and applied to the payment of any of my debts.

ITEM VIII.

I hereby nominate, constitute and appoint *M J Otey* of *Grainda, Ok* as executor of this my last will and testament and direct that he give bond as provided by law.

IN WITNESS WHEREOF, I have hereunto subscribed my name in the presence of these witnesses, who at my request and in my presence have subscribed their names to this my last will and testament.

Dated at Arkansas City, Kansas, this *30* day of August, 1913.

Charles Edmond Fuller

We, the undersigned witnesses to the above and foregoing will of Charles Fuller, consisting of Five (5) pages, and consisting of Items One (1) to Eight (8), both inclusive, do hereby certify that the testator signed the above and foregoing will in our presence after having had the same read over to him, and that the said testator in our presence acknowledged the execution of the same and declared to us, the attesting witnesses, that the above and foregoing instrument was and is his last will and testament, and we at his direction and request and in his presence, and in the presence of each other, have hereunto subscribed our names as attesting witnesses and annexed our address hereto.

Dated and done this *30* day of August, 1913, at Arkansas City, Kansas.

NAME   RESIDENCE

R Claude Young   *Arkansas City, Kans.*
Lena B Grant   *Arkansas City, Kan.*

Department of The Interior,
Office of Indian Affairs, Washington,
                    MAR 21 1916

It is respectfully recommended that the within will be approved pursuant to the provisions of Section 8 of the Act of April 18, 1912 (37 Stat. L. 86, 88) in so far as it relates to property under the Jurisdiction of the United States.

Respectfully,
EB Meritt
Assistant Commissioner

Department of The Interior
Office of The Secretary MAR 29 1916

The within will is hereby approved pursuant to the provisions of Section 8 of the Act of April 18, 1912 (37 Stat. L. 86, 88) in so far as it relates to property under the Jurisdiction of the United States.

Bo Sweeney
Assistant Secretary

▲▼▲▼▲▼▲▼▲▼▲▼▲▼

DAY COMES OUT

Original
WILL

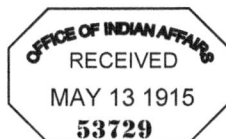

OFFICE OF INDIAN AFFAIRS
RECEIVED
MAY 13 1915
53729

    I, **Day Comes Out** of Pine Ridge Agency, South Dakota, Allottee number **6458**, do hereby make and declare this to be my last will and testament, in accordance with Section 2 of the Act of June 25, 1910, (36 stat. 855-858) and Act of February 14, 1913, (Public No. 381), hereby revoking all former wills made by me:

1. I hereby direct that as soon as possible after my decease, that all my debts, funeral and testamentary expenses be paid out of my personal estate.

2. I give and devise my allotment on the Pine Ridge Reservation, South Dakota, described as follows:

N/2 of Sec. 17, T 36 N, R 44 W. 320 acres

in the following manner:

NW/4 of Sec. 17, T 36 N. R 44 W, to my son, Charles Good Voice Iron.

NE/4 of Sec. 17, T 36 N, R 44 W, to my daughter, Red Door.

~~3. I give and bequeath all of my personal property of whatsoever nature and wheresoever situated unto~~ *(Marked out on original.)*

4. All the rest of my property, real or personal, now possessed or hereafter acquired, of whatsoever nature and wheresoever situated, I hereby give, devise and bequeath unto

One horse to my daughter, Red Door. The rest of my property consisting of an old wagon, to my husband, Runs Above.

In witness whereof I have hereunto set my hand this **7th** day of **May** 1915   **her**

Day Comes Out [thumb print]

mark

The above statement was, this **7th** day of **May** 1915, signed and published by **Day Comes Out** as **her** last will and testament, in the joint presence of the undersigned, the said **Day Comes Out** then being of sound and vigorous mid and free from any constraint or compulsion; whereupon we, being without any interest in the matter other than friendship, and being well acquainted with **her** but not members of **her** family, immediately subscribed our names hereto in the presence of each other and of the said testator, for the purpose of attesting the said will, as .... requested us to do. *(Note: "........." are areas left blank on the original.)*

	Post Office Address
H E Wright	**Pine Ridge, S. D.**
OC Ross	**Pine Ridge, S. D.**

Pine Ridge, South Dakota.
NOV 29 1915

Indian Wills, 1911 – 1921 Book Three
Records of The Bureau of Indian Affairs

I hereby certify that I have fully inquired into the mental competency of the Indian signing the above will; the circumstances attending the execution of the will; the influence that may have induced its execution, and the names of those entitled to share in the estate under the law of descent in South Dakota: reasons for the disposition of the property proposed by the will differing from disposition had the property descended by operation of law.

I respectfully forward this will with the recommendation that it be ......approved.

John R Brennan
Supt. & Spl. Disb. Agent.

Department of The Interior,
Office of Indian Affairs, Washington,
FEB 19 1916

The within will is hereby recommended for approval in accordance with the Act of June 25, 1910 (36 Stats. L., 855-6) as amended by Act of February 14, 1913 (37 Stats. L., 678), so far as relates to property held in trust by the United States.

Respectfully,
EB Meritt
Assistant Commissioner

Department of The Interior
Office of The Secretary FEB 21 1916

The within will is hereby approved in accordance with the Act of June 25, 1910 (36 Stats. L., 855-6) as amended by Act of February 14, 1913 (37 Stats. L., 678),

A A Jones
Assistant Secretary

▲▼▲▼▲▼▲▼▲▼▲▼▲▼

OFFICE OF INDIAN AFFAIRS
RECEIVED
OCT 6- 1916
104351

LEVI JACKSON
Copy of the will of Levi Jackson.

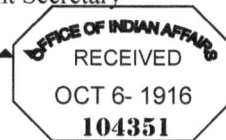

I, Levi Jackson, of the township of Denver in the County of Isabella and State of Michigan, being of sound mind and memory, do make, publish and declare this to be my last will and testament, in manner following, viz:

143

First, I will and direct that all my just debts and funeral expenses be paid in full;

Second, I give and bequeath to my uncle, Jacob Jackson, and Daniel Jackson, in equal shares, all of my estate, both real and personal.

Lastly, I hereby revoke all former will by me at any time made.

In witness whereof I have hereunto set my hand and seal this 16th day of September in the year of our Lord one thousand nine hundred and ten.

(Signed) Levi Jackson (his mark)
(Seal)
(Signed) Angee Pashinea, (witness to mark)

On this sixteenth day of September, A. D. 1910.

NE/4 of SE/4 Sect 8 Twp. of Denver in the County of Isabella and State of Michigan.

Signed the foregoing instrument in our presence and declared it to be his last will and testament, and as witness thereof, we do no, at his request, and in the presence of each other, hereunto subscribe our names.

(Signed) Jennie Arnot, residing at her home
(Signed) Louis C Nowlen   "   "   "   "
(Signed) Thomas M Proat,
Township Clerk

I hereby certify that the above is a true and correct copy of the will of Levi Jackson, as it appears on the records at the Court House, Mt. Pleasant, Michigan.

R.A. Cochran
Superintendent.

104351-16.
80702-16

Department of The Interior,
Office of Indian Affairs, Washington,
NOV 14 1916

Indian Wills, 1911 – 1921 Book Three
Records of The Bureau of Indian Affairs

It is respectfully recommended that the alienation of the allotment by devise through the within will of Levi Jackson, be approved subject to the continuation of the restriction against alienation without the consent of the Secretary of the Interior.

Respectfully,
EB Meritt
Assistant Commissioner

Department of The Interior
Office of The Secretary NOV 20 1916

In conformity with the terms of the patent issued therefore under the provisions of the treaty of October 18, 1864 (14 Stat. L. 657), the alienation by devise of the allotment involved herein, through the within will of Levi Jackson, sole heir of Julia Jackson, is hereby approved, subject to the continuation of the restriction against alienation without the consent of the Secretary of the Interior.

Bo Sweeney
Assistant Secretary

▲▼▲▼▲▼▲▼▲▼▲▼▲▼

LITTLE CROW

Original
WILL

OFFICE OF INDIAN AFFAIRS
RECEIVED
DEC 22 1915
136397

I, **Little Crow** of Pine Ridge Agency, South Dakota, Allottee number 1691 do hereby make and declare this to be my last will and testament, in accordance with Section 2 of the Act of June 25, 1910, (36 stat. 855-858) and Act of February 14, 1913, (Public No. 381), hereby revoking all former wills made by me:

1. I hereby direct that as soon as possible after my decease, that all my debts, funeral and testamentary expenses be paid out of my personal estate.

2. I give and devise my allotment on the Pine Ridge Reservation, South Dakota, described as follows:

N1/2 of NW1/4 Sec. 8, T. 35 N/, Range 45 W; and SW1/4 and W1/2 of SE1/4 Sec. 12, T37N, Range 40 W. of the 6th P.M. in South

Dakota; and N1/2 Sec. 12, T37N, Range 40 W.. of the 6th P.M. in South Dakota.

in the following manner:

To Emma Stirk, the North 1/2 and SW1/4 and W1/2 of SE1/4, Sec. 12, T37N, Range 40W containing 560 acres.

To Good Cow, my wife, Mary Hand, my daughter, and Maggie Gray Blanket, my daughter, the balance of my allotment, share and share alike, described as follows: N1/2 of NW1/4 Sec. 8, T 35N, Range 45 W, of the 6th P.M. in South Dakota, containing 80 acres.

3. I give and bequeath all of my personal property of whatsoever nature and wheresoever situated unto

Good Cow, my wife, Mary Hand, my daughter, and Maggie Gray Blanket, my daughter, share and share alike.

4. All the rest of my property, real or personal, now possessed or hereafter acquired, of whatsoever nature and wheresoever situated, I hereby give, devise and bequeath unto

Good Cow, my wife, Mary Hand, my daughter, and Maggie Gray Blanket, my daughter, share and share alike.

In witness whereof I have hereunto set my hand this **31st** day of **May** 191*1*

Little Crow [thumb print]

The above statement was, this *31st* day of *May* 191*1* signed and published by **Little Crow** as **his** last will and testament, in the joint presence of the undersigned, the said **Little Crow** then being of sound and vigorous mid and free from any constraint or compulsion; whereupon we, being without any interest in the matter other than friendship, and being well acquainted with **him** but not members of **his** family, immediately subscribed our names hereto in the presence of each other and of the said testator, for the purpose of attesting the said will, as **he** requested us to do. **And that I, Adrian M Landman, at the request of Little Crow, signed his name in ink and he affixed his thumb mark.**

Post Office Address

(Signature Illegible) **PINE RIDGE AGENCY, S. DAK.**

(Signature Illegible)

Pine Ridge, South Dakota.

Apr 23 1914

    I hereby certify that I have fully inquired into the mental competency of the Indian signing the above will; the circumstances attending the execution of the will; the influence that may have induced its execution, and the names of those entitled to share in the estate under the law of descent in South Dakota: reasons for the disposition of the property proposed by the will differing from disposition had the property descended by operation of law.

    I respectfully forward this will with the recommendation that it be .....approved.

John R Brennan
Supt. & Spl. Disb. Agent.

Department of The Interior,
Office of Indian Affairs, Washington,

MAY 28 1914

It is recommended that the within will be approved pursuant to the provisions of the Act of June 25, 1910 (36 Stats. L., 855-6) as amended by Act of February 14, 1913 (37 Stats. L., 678).

Respectfully,
EB Meritt
Assistant Commissioner

Department of The Interior
Office of The Secretary JUN -1 1914

The within will is hereby approved pursuant to the provisions of the Act of June 25, 1910 (36 Stats. L., 855-6) as amended by Act of February 14, 1913 (37 Stats. L., 678).

Bo Sweeney
Assistant Secretary

▲▼▲▼▲▼▲▼▲▼▲▼▲▼

PIPE ON HEAD

OFFICE OF INDIAN AFFAIRS
RECEIVED
JAN 24 1916
7592

Original
WILL

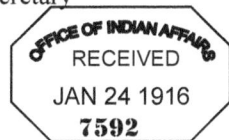

Indian Wills, 1911 – 1921 Book Three
Records of The Bureau of Indian Affairs

I, **Pipe On Head** of Pine Ridge Agency, South Dakota, Allottee number **6164** do hereby make and declare this to be my last will and testament, in accordance with Section 2 of the Act of June 25, 1910, (36 stat. 855-858) and Act of February 14, 1913, (Public No. 381), hereby revoking all former wills made by me:

1. I hereby direct that as soon as possible after my decease, that all my debts, funeral and testamentary expenses be paid out of my personal estate.

2. I give and devise my allotment on the Pine Ridge Reservation, South Dakota, described as follows:

S1/2 of N1/2 of Sec. 29 & S1/2 of N1/2 & S1/2 of Sec. 28 T. 37 N., R. 46 W. of the 6th P.M. in South Dakota.

in the following manner:

To my wife Lucinda I bequeath the S1/2 of N1/2 of Sec. 29 T. 37 N., R. 46 W. of the 6th P.M. cont. 160 A.

To my son James Pipe on Head I bequeath the S1/2 of Sec. 28 T. 37 N., R. 46 W of the 6th P.M. in South Dakota, containing 320 acres.

To my grandchild Susie Pipe On Head daughter of James Pipe On Head I bequeath the S1/2 of N1/2 of Sec. 28 T. 37 N., R. 46 W. of the 6th P.M. in South Dakota containing 160 acres.

3. I give and bequeath all of my personal property of whatsoever nature and wheresoever situated unto

To my son James Pipe On Head, all, with exception of one team wagon & harness which I give to my wife Lucinda Pipe On Head also I bequeath to her a house

4. All the rest of my property, real or personal, now possessed or hereafter acquired, of whatsoever nature and wheresoever situated, I hereby give, devise and bequeath unto

To my wife Lucinda Pipe On Head all.

In witness whereof I have hereunto set my hand this **27** day of **April** 19**15**

		his
Witnesses to signature by mark:		[thumb print]
L L Smith	*Pipe On Head*	*mark*
Farmer, Oglala, S. D.		
Mark R Eagle		
Ass't Farmer, Oglala, S.D.		

The above statement was, this **27** day of **April** 1915 signed and published by **Pipe On Head** as **his** last will and testament, in the joint presence of the undersigned, the said **Pipe On Head** then being of sound and vigorous mid and free from any constraint or compulsion; whereupon we, being without any interest in the matter other than friendship, and being well acquainted with **him** but not members of **his** family, immediately subscribed our names hereto in the presence of each other and of the said testator, for the purpose of attesting the said will, as **he** requested us to do.

Post Office Address

L L Smith **Oglala, S. D.**

Mark R Eagle " " "

Pine Ridge, South Dakota.

AUG 25 1915

I hereby certify that I have fully inquired into the mental competency of the Indian signing the above will; the circumstances attending the execution of the will; the influence that may have induced its execution, and the names of those entitled to share in the estate under the law of descent in South Dakota: reasons for the disposition of the property proposed by the will differing from disposition had the property descended by operation of law.

I respectfully forward this will with the recommendation that it be .....approved.

John R Brennan
Supt. & Spl. Disb. Agent.

Department of The Interior,
Office of Indian Affairs, Washington,

OCT 21 1915

It is recommended that the within will be approved in accordance with the Act of June 25, 1910 (36 Stats. L., 855-6) as amended by Act of February 14, 1913 (37 Stats. L., 678).

Indian Wills, 1911 – 1921 Book Three
Records of The Bureau of Indian Affairs

Respectfully,
EB Meritt
Assistant Commissioner

Department of The Interior
Office of The Secretary

The within will is hereby approved in accordance with the Act of June 25, 1910 (36 Stats. L., 855-6) as amended by Act of February 14, 1913 (37 Stats. L., 678).

Bo Sweeney
Assistant Secretary

▲▼▲▼▲▼▲▼▲▼▲▼▲▼▲▼

FRANK JARVIS

Original
WILL

I, **Frank Jarvis** of Pine Ridge Agency, South Dakota, Allottee number **4158** do hereby make and declare this to be my last will and testament, in accordance with Section 2 of the Act of June 25, 1910, (36 stat. 855-858) and Act of February 14, 1913, (Public No. 381), hereby revoking all former wills made by me:

1. I hereby direct that as soon as possible after my decease, that all my debts, funeral and testamentary expenses be paid out of my personal estate.

2. I give and devise my allotment **and inherited land** on the Pine Ridge Reservation, South Dakota, described as follows:

My allotment, all of Sec. 25, T 41, R 34 W, 6th P.M, S.D. 640 A.

Undivided half interest in Allot. No. 4159, W/2 of Sec. 36, T 41, R 34 W of 6th P.M., S.D., 320 A.
in the following manner:

SE/4 of Sec. 25, T 41, R 34, to my mother, Grace Jarvis.

NE/4 of Sec. 25, T 41, R 34, to my son, Giles Jarvis.

Indian Wills, 1911 – 1921 Book Three
Records of The Bureau of Indian Affairs

W/2 of Sec. 25, T 41, R 34, to my wife, Lizzie Jarvis.

Undivided half interest in @/3 of Sec. 36, T 41, R 34, to my son, Giles Jarvis.

3. I give and bequeath all of my personal property of whatsoever nature and wheresoever situated unto

One ID mare, one heifer, one wagon, and one set of harness to Lizzie Jarvis, my wife.

4. All the rest of my property, real or personal, now possessed or hereafter acquired, of whatsoever nature and wheresoever situated, I hereby give, devise and bequeath unto

my wife, Lizzie Jarvis.

In witness whereof I have hereunto set my hand this **2d** day of **March 1915**.

Frank Jarvis

The above statement was, this **2d** day of **March** 1915 signed and published by **Frank Jarvis** as **his** last will and testament, in the joint presence of the undersigned, the said **Frank Jarvis** then being of sound and vigorous mid and free from any constraint or compulsion; whereupon we, being without any interest in the matter other than friendship, and being well acquainted with **him** but not members of **his** family, immediately subscribed our names hereto in the presence of each other and of the said testator, for the purpose of attesting the said will, as **he** requested us to do.

	Post Office Address
H E Wright	**Pine Ridge, S. D.**
OC Ross	**Pine Ridge, S. D.**

Pine Ridge, South Dakota.
Feb 17 1917

I hereby certify that I have fully inquired into the mental competency of the Indian signing the above will; the circumstances attending the execution of the will; the influence that may have induced its execution, and the names of those entitled to share in the estate under the law of descent in South Dakota: reasons for the disposition of the property proposed by the will differing from disposition had the property descended by operation of law.

I respectfully forward this will with the recommendation that it be .....approved.

John R Brennan
Supt. & Spl. Disb. Agent.

Department of The Interior,
Office of Indian Affairs, Washington,
FEB 19 1916

The within will is hereby recommended for approval in accordance with the Act of June 25, 1910 (36 Stats. L., 855-6) as amended by Act of February 14, 1913 (37 Stats. L., 678), so far as relates to property held in trust by the United States.

Respectfully,
EB Meritt
Assistant Commissioner

Department of The Interior
Office of The Secretary FEB 21 1916

The within will is hereby approved in accordance with the Act of June 25, 1910 (36 Stats. L., 855-6) as amended by Act of February 14, 1913 (37 Stats. L., 678), so far as relates to property held in trust by the United States.

Bo Sweeney
Assistant Secretary

LOUIS FEW TAILS

OFFICE OF INDIAN AFFAIRS
RECEIVED
FEB 26 1916
21057

Original
WILL

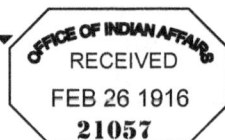

I, **Louis Few Tails** of Pine Ridge Agency, South Dakota, Allottee number **1530** do hereby make and declare this to be my last will and testament, in accordance with Section 2 of the Act of June 25, 1910, (36 stat. 855-858) and Act of February 14, 1913, (Public No. 381), hereby revoking all former wills made by me:

1. I hereby direct that as soon as possible after my decease, that all my debts, funeral and testamentary expenses be paid out of my personal

estate.

2. I give and devise my allotment on the Pine Ridge Reservation, South Dakota, described as follows:

The S/2 of Sec. 9 in Twp. 40 N of Range 41 west of the 6th P.M., South Dakota, containing 320 acres.

in the following manner:

To my mother, Brings Horses; my brothers: Samuel and Eugene Few Tails and William Eagle Shirt, my entire allotment to be divided equally between them.

3. I give and bequeath all of my personal property of whatsoever nature and wheresoever situated unto

To my mother, Brings Horses: One I.D. mare.

To my brother, Samuel Few Tails: one sorrel horse.

To my brother, Eugene Few Tails: one black mare.

4. All the rest of my property, real or personal, now possessed or hereafter acquired, of whatsoever nature and wheresoever situated, I hereby give, devise and bequeath unto

To my mother, Brings Horses; my brothers: Samuel and Eugene Few Tails and William Eagle Shirt, in equal shares.

In witness whereof I have hereunto set my hand this **20th** day of **October 1914**   *his mark*
                                                Louis Few Tails [thumb print]

The above statement was, this **20th** day of **October** 1914, signed and published by **Louis Few Tails** as **his** last will and testament, in the joint presence of the undersigned, the said **Louis Few Tails** then being of sound and vigorous mid and free from any constraint or compulsion; whereupon we, being without any interest in the matter other than friendship, and being well acquainted with **him** but not members of **his** family, immediately subscribed our names hereto in the presence of each other and of the said testator, for the purpose of attesting the said will, as **he** requested us to do, **his name being signed by George A. Trotter, one of the witnesses, at his request.**

	Post Office Address
George A Trotter	**Kyle, South Dakota.**
Peter Chiefeagle	**Kyle, South Dakota.**

Pine Ridge, South Dakota.
DEC 1 1915

I hereby certify that I have fully inquired into the mental competency of the Indian signing the above will; the circumstances attending the execution of the will; the influence that may have induced its execution, and the names of those entitled to share in the estate under the law of descent in South Dakota: reasons for the disposition of the property proposed by the will differing from disposition had the property descended by operation of law.

I respectfully forward this will with the recommendation that it be *dis* approved.

John R Brennan
Supt. & Spl. Disb. Agent.

Department of The Interior,
Office of Indian Affairs, Washington,
JAN 27 1916

It is recommended that the within will be approved in accordance with the Act of June 25, 1910 (36 Stats. L., 855-6) as amended by Act of February 14, 1913 (37 Stats. L., 678).

Respectfully,
EB Meritt
Assistant Commissioner

Department of The Interior
Office of The Secretary
JAN 28 1916

The within will is hereby approved in accordance with the Act of June 25, 1910 (36 Stats. L., 855-6) as amended by Act of February 14, 1913 (37 Stats. L., 678).

Bo Sweeney
Assistant Secretary

▲▼▲▼▲▼▲▼▲▼▲▼▲▼

HENRY YELLOW THIGH or SICANZI

OFFICE OF INDIAN AFFAIRS
RECEIVED
MAR 6- 1916
24669

Indian Wills, 1911 – 1921 Book Three
Records of The Bureau of Indian Affairs

LAST WILL And TESTAMENT OF HENRY YELLOW

THIGH OR SICANZI.

I, Henry Yellow Thigh or Sicanzi, being of sound and disposing mind and memory and wishing to make a final disposition of my property, do hereby publish and declare the following to be my last will and testament, and do hereby revoke all other wills and codicils heretofore by me made.

My only heir at law is my son Simon Vassar, and I am a widower. I wish to leave all of my property and hereby bequeath and devise to said Simon Vassar all of my property, which is more specifically described as follows:

I am allottee No. 330 on the Cheyenne River Indian Reservation, South Dakota, and this allotment is described as All of Section twenty-nine (29), Township fifteen (15), Range thirty (30), containing six hundred forty (640) acres.

The Secretary of the Interior determined me to be an heir to an undivided 11/54 interest in the estate of Ground Hog, deceased Cheyenne River Sioux allottee No. 102, and this allotment is described as follows: SE/4 of Sec. 12, N/2 of NE/4 & N/2 of NW/4 of Sec. 13; NW/4 & W/2 of SW/4 of Sec. 34, T. 16 N., R 30 E; & NW/4 of NW/4 of Sec. 18, & W/2 of W/2 of SW/4 of Sec. 7, T. 16 N., R. 31 E., containing 640 acres.

The Secretary of the Interior determined me to be an heir to an undivided 1/2 interest in the estate of Alice Yellow Thigh, deceased Cheyenne River Sioux allottee No. 2649, and this allotment is described as follows: N/2 of Sec. 32, T. 15 N., R. 30 E., containing 320 acres.

I further bequeath and devise any other property, real or personal, which I may be found entitled to at the time of my death, to said Simon Vassar. Simon Vassar is my son and he has agreed to take care of me during the rest of my life. Should Simon Vassar fail to keep this promise to take care of me during the rest of my life, I hereby declare that this will shall be null and void.

IN TESTIMONY WHEREOF I have hereunto set my thumb mark and seal this third day of January, in the year of our Lord 1916, my name

155

being written in at my request by *Penn Garfield*

His thumb

Witnesses to thumb mark: (SEAL) *Henry Yellow Thigh* [thumb print]
    Penn Garfield   mark.
    George Nichols

      SIGNED, SEALED, PUBLISHED, AND DECLARED by said Henry Yellow Thigh or Sicanzi in our presence, as and for his last will and testament, and at his request, and in his presence, and in the presence of each other, we have hereunto subscribed our names as attesting witnesses thereto.

      (name)   *Penn Garfield*
      (Residence) Cheyenne Agency, S. D.
      (name)   *George Nichols*
      (Residence) Cheyenne Agency, S. D.

Department of The Interior,
Office of Indian Affairs, Washington,
                FEB 16 1916
It is recommended that the within will be approved in accordance with the Act of June 25, 1910 (36 Stats. L., 855-6) as amended by Act of February 14, 1913 (37 Stats. L., 678).

               Respectfully,
               EB Meritt
               Assistant Commissioner

Department of The Interior
Office of The Secretary
             FEB 17 1916
The within will is hereby approved in accordance with the Act of June 25, 1910 (36 Stats. L., 855-6) as amended by Act of February 14, 1913 (37 Stats. L., 678).

               Bo Sweeney
               Assistant Secretary

▲▼▲▼▲▼▲▼▲▼▲▼▲▼▲▼

SUSIE PARTS-HIS-HAIR

OFFICE OF INDIAN AFFAIRS
RECEIVED
JAN 17 1916
5094

        Original
        WILL

Indian Wills, 1911 – 1921 Book Three
Records of The Bureau of Indian Affairs

I, **Susie Parts-his-hair** of Pine Ridge Agency, South Dakota, Allottee number **1386** do hereby make and declare this to be my last will and testament, in accordance with Section 2 of the Act of June 25, 1910, (36 stat. 855-858) and Act of February 14, 1913, (Public No. 381), hereby revoking all former wills made by me:

1. I hereby direct that as soon as possible after my decease, that all my debts, funeral and testamentary expenses be paid out of my personal estate.

2. I give and devise my allotment on the Pine Ridge Reservation, South Dakota, described as follows:

The E/2 of Section 24 in Twp. 39 N. of Range 42 west of the 6th P.M., and the W/2 of Section 9 in Twp. 38 N. of Range 41 west of the Sixth Principal Meridian, South Dakota, containing 640 acres.

in the following manner:

to my son, Amos Parts-his-hair: the SE/4 of Sec. 24 in Twp. 39 N. of Range 42

to my daughter, Ada Parts-his-hair: the NE/4 of Sec. 24 in Twp. 39 N. of Range 42

to my son Ephriam Parts-his-hair; my daughter, Emma Parts-his-hair; and my grand-son, Moses Parts-his-hair: the N/2 of Section 9 in Twp. 38 N. of Range 41 west of the 6th P.M., in equal shares. The same to be sold and the money divided or kept by them if they so desire.

3. I give and bequeath all of my personal property of whatsoever nature and wheresoever situated ~~unto~~ **in the following manner:**

To my daughter, Ada Parts-his-hair: one issue mare, wagon, harness.

To my daughter, Emma Parts-his-hair: one issue mare.

4. All the rest of my property, real ~~or personal~~, now possessed or

hereafter acquired, of whatsoever nature and wheresoever situated, I hereby give, devise and bequeath unto

my sons, **Ephriam** and **Amos Parts-his-hair**, my daughters, **Ada** and **Emma Parts-his-hair**, and my grand-son, **Moses Parts-his-hair**, in equal shares.

In witness whereof I have hereunto set my hand this **4th** day of **March 1915**
her mark
Susie Parts-his-hair [thumb print]

The above statement was, this **4th** day of **March** 1915 signed and published by **Susie Parts-his-hair** as **her** last will and testament, in the joint presence of the undersigned, the said **Susie Parts-his-hair** then being of sound and vigorous mid and free from any constraint or compulsion; whereupon we, being without any interest in the matter other than friendship, and being well acquainted with **her** but not members of **her** family, immediately subscribed our names hereto in the presence of each other and of the said testator, for the purpose of attesting the said will, as **she** requested us to do, **her name being signed by George A. Trotter, one of the witnesses, at her request.**

Post Office Address

George A Trotter   **Kyle, South Dakota.**
Peter Chiefeagle   **Kyle, South Dakota.**

Pine Ridge, South Dakota.
Jan 18 1916

I hereby certify that I have fully inquired into the mental competency of the Indian signing the above will; the circumstances attending the execution of the will; the influence that may have induced its execution, and the names of those entitled to share in the estate under the law of descent in South Dakota: reasons for the disposition of the property proposed by the will differing from disposition had the property descended by operation of law.

I respectfully forward this will with the recommendation that it be *dis* approved.

John R Brennan
Supt. & Spl. Disb. Agent.

Department of The Interior,
Office of Indian Affairs, Washington,

Indian Wills, 1911 – 1921 Book Three
Records of The Bureau of Indian Affairs

MAR 10 1916

It is recommended that the within will be approved in accordance with the Act of June 25, 1910 (36 Stats. L., 855-6) as amended by Act of February 14, 1913 (37 Stats. L., 678).

Respectfully,

EB Meritt

Assistant Commissioner

Department of The Interior
Office of The Secretary
MAR 21 1916

The within will is hereby approved in accordance with the Act of June 25, 1910 (36 Stats. L., 855-6) as amended by Act of February 14, 1913 (37 Stats. L., 678).

Bo Sweeney

Assistant Secretary

▲▼▲▼▲▼▲▼▲▼▲▼▲▼

<u>JOSEPH MERRICK</u>

Will

I Joseph Merrick, of the Omaha Tribe of Indians and a resident of Thurston County, Nebraska, being of sound mind and memory, do hereby and by these presents make and publish and declare this instrument to be my last will and testament hereby revoking any former will which I may have made.

First

I give and bequeath and devise unto my daughter Mary Merrick Walker the West 1/2 of the WW1/4[sic] of Section 12, Township 25, and Range 8 East of the Sixth Principal Meridian and containing 80 acres.

Second

I give and bequeath and devise unto my daughter Mattie Merrick White the East 1/2 of the North West 1/4 of Section 12, Township 25, and Range 8 East of Sixth Principal Meridian and containing 80 acres.

Third

Indian Wills, 1911 – 1921 Book Three
Records of The Bureau of Indian Affairs

I give and bequeath and devise unto my daughter Mabel Merrick all money of which I may be possessed of at the time of my death held in trust by the Superintendent of the Omaha Agency.

In testimony whereof, I have hereunto set my hand this first day of June 1915, in the presence of   His

Joseph Merrick [thumb print]

Witnesses   mark
Silas Wood
Maggie Merrick

We the undersigned, do hereby certify that we have signed the above instrument as subscribing witnesses in the presence of each other and at his request and said instrument was explained to him said testator in our presence and he understood the same and said testator did thereupon sign the same.

Witnesses
Silas Wood
Maggie Merrick

Subscribed and sworn to before me this first day of June 1915.

Axel Johnson
Supt Omaha Agency

Department of The Interior,
Office of Indian Affairs, Washington,
APR 13 1916
It is recommended that the within will be approved in accordance with the Act of June 25, 1910 (36 Stats. L., 855-6) as amended by Act of February 14, 1913 (37 Stats. L., 678).

Respectfully,
EB Meritt
Assistant Commissioner

Department of The Interior
Office of The Secretary
APR 14 1916
The within will is hereby approved in accordance with the Act of June 25, 1910 (36 Stats. L., 855-6) as amended by Act of February 14, 1913 (37 Stats. L., 678).

Bo Sweeney
Assistant Secretary

▲▼▲▼▲▼▲▼▲▼▲▼▲▼▲▼

GEORGE LESLIE

LAST WILL AND TESTAMENT OF GEORGE LESLIE.

I, George Leslie, of Muckleshoot Reservation, Cushman Agency, Washington, of the age of about 51 years, and being of sound and disposing mind and memory, and not acting under duress, menace, fraud or undue influence of any person whatever, do make, publish and declare this my LAST WILL AND TESTAMENT, in manner following, that is to say:

First:-- I hereby direct that all my funeral expense be first paid.

Second:-- I give and bequeath to my son Cain Leslie the sum of ten dollars ($10.00)

Third:-- I give and bequeath to my daughter Emma the sum of ten dollars ($10.00)

Fourth:-- I give and bequeath to my wife Alice Leslie all of the rest of the money to my credit in the bank and the money that will come from the sale of the land and now secured by a mortgage.

I hereby appoint my wife, Alice Leslie, Executrix of this my last will and testament, and hereby revoke all former wills by me made.

In witness whereof, I have hereunto set my hand and seal this *8* day of July 1915   His
                                         George Leslie Thumb
Witnesses to mark   mark.
   Alexander J Porter
   Chas A. Reynolds

The foregoing instrument, consisting of this page only, was at the date thereof, to-wit: on the *8* day of July 1915 by the said George Leslie, signed, sealed, published as and declared to be his Last Will and Testament, in presence of us, who at his request and in his presence and

161

in the presence of each other, have subscribed our names as witnesses thereto.

Alexander J Porter   Residing at ~~Muckleshoot, Res'n~~, Auburn, Wash

Chas A Reynolds   Residing at Muckleshoot, Res'n, Auburn, Wash

Department of The Interior,
Office of Indian Affairs, Washington,
JUN 12 1916

The within will is hereby recommended for approval in accordance with the Act of June 25, 1910 (36 Stats. L., 855-6) as amended by Act of February 14, 1913 (37 Stats. L., 678).

> Respectfully,
> *EB Meritt*
> Assistant Commissioner

Department of The Interior
Office of The Secretary   JUN 26 1916

The within will is hereby approved in accordance with the Act of June 25, 1910 (36 Stats. L., 855-6) as amended by Act of February 14, 1913 (37 Stats. L., 678), with the provision that no right of an Executor is recognized in connection therewith.

> *Bo Sweeney*
> Assistant Secretary

▲▼▲▼▲▼▲▼▲▼▲▼▲▼▲

GEORGE HUNTER

LAST WILL AND TESTAMENT OF

> OFFICE OF INDIAN AFFAIRS
> RECEIVED
> MAY 23 1916
> 56024

GEORGE HUNTER.

KNOW ALL MEN BY THESE PRESENTS:-   That I, the undersigned, George Thunder, being of sound mind and disposing memory, do hereby make and declare this my last will and testament.

First:--I hereby direct that all of my just debts, including my last illness and funeral expenses be paid out of any moneys belonging to my estate.

Indian Wills, 1911 – 1921 Book Three
Records of The Bureau of Indian Affairs

Second:--to Wilber Harden, whom I have adopted as my son after the manner of the Indians, I give, devise and bequeath that portion of my allotment upon the Winnebago Reservation, Nebraska, described as Lots three and six Section nineteen (19), Township twenty-six (26) North of Range nine (9) East of the 6th Principal Meridian, containing according to the United States Government Survey Thirty-nine and ninety-two hundredth (39.92) acres. The same to be his forever.

Third:--To Julia Harden whom I have adopted as my daughter according to the custom of Indians, I give, devise, and bequeath that portion of my allotment upon the Winnebago Reservation, Nebraska, described as the Southeast Quarter of the Northwest Quarter of Section nineteen (19), Township twenty-sic (26) North of Range nine (9) East of the 6th P.M., containing according to the United States Government Survey forty acres, the same to be hers forever.

Fourth:--What ever Heirship lands I may have and whatever moneys I may have after my debts are paid I give, devise and bequeath to said Wilber Harden and to said Julia Harden in equal shares. The same to be theirs forever. His

Signed George Thunder [thumb print]

Mark.

Witness to Mark.

Addie Boncher

Lucy C Palmer, Asst. Clerk

The said testator at this time signed his name to the above and foregoing instrument in the presence of the undersigned, and at the same time declared the same to be his last will and testament and we, at his request, and in his presence and in the presence of each other, do hereby sign our names hereto as attesting witnesses.

Winnebago Agency, Nebr.,   *Hugh Hunter*

    May 18, 1916.   *Lucy C. Palmer*

Department of The Interior,
Office of Indian Affairs, Washington,
JUN -6 1916

The within will is hereby recommended for approval in accordance with the Act of June 25, 1910 (36 Stats. L., 855-6) as amended by Act of February 14, 1913 (37 Stats. L., 678).

Indian Wills, 1911 – 1921 Book Three
Records of The Bureau of Indian Affairs

Respectfully,

EB Meritt

Assistant Commissioner

Department of The Interior

Office of The Secretary JUN 19 1916

The within will is hereby approved in accordance with the Act of June 25, 1910 (36 Stats. L., 855-6) as amended by Act of February 14, 1913 (37 Stats. L., 678).

Bo Sweeney

Assistant Secretary

OFFICE OF INDIAN AFFAIRS
RECEIVED
(Date Illegible)
132771

▲▼▲▼▲▼▲▼▲▼▲▼▲▼

MRS. McFADDEN WHYAMA

LAST WILL OF Mrs. McFadden Whyama, Allottee No. 455.

Colorado River Reservation,

Parker, Arizona.

This will, made this 3rd day of November, A.D., 1913, while I am in my right mind and in full bodily vigor, is made for the purpose of giving to the persons named herein the various items of my estate, to wit:

Item. My undivided interest in the allotment of Joe Whyama, my deceased husband, father of Jim Welsh, I desire to be given to the said Jim Welsh as a voluntary reimbursing for the expense to which he has been during the last five years for keeping myself and my husband, - his father, - and for the care and kindness shown at all times. Joe Whyama's allotment is described as W/2W/2NW/4SW/4 of Sec. 25, T/9, R. 20., No. 454.

Item. My own allotment, described as Lot 2 and the W 5 chs. of the S 10 chs. of lot 1, all in Sec. 11, Twp. 9, N., Range 20, West, containing in all 9.57 acres, I desire to give to Charley Elmore, my nephew. This I do for the reason that I have no living children nor grand children, and this is my favorite living relative.

Item. All my personal effects that I may have at the time of my death, of whatever nature, I desire to give to the above named Charley Elmore, for the reasons set forth above.

Indian Wills, 1911 – 1921 Book Three
Records of The Bureau of Indian Affairs

Done at the Colorado River Agency, this 3rd day of November, A. D., 1913, of my free will, and without any of the interested parties herein, using any influence, whatever.

Her
Mrs. McFadden Whyama [thumb print]

Witnesses: mark

    George Sands
    Carl Scott

    I certify that I have well and faithfully interpreted the above from the Mohave to the English and that the above text sets forth the meaning of the said Mrs. McFadden Whyama, as communicated to me.

Randall Booth
Interpreter.

Department of The Interior,
Office of Indian Affairs, Washington,
        JUN 19 1916

It is recommended that the within will be approved under the Act of June 25, 1910 (36 Stats. L., 855-6) as amended by Act of February 14, 1913 (37 Stats. L., 678).

Respectfully
EB Meritt
Assistant Commissioner

Department of The Interior
Office of The Secretary   JUN 22 1916

The within will is hereby approved under the Act of June 25, 1910 (36 Stats. L., 855-6) as amended by Act of February 14, 1913 (37 Stats. L., 678).

Bo Sweeney
Assistant Secretary

▲▼▲▼▲▼▲▼▲▼▲▼▲▼▲▼

WAH-TSA-ME

OFFICE OF INDIAN AFFAIRS
RECEIVED
APR 18 1916
42100

W-I-L-L

    I, Wah-tsa-me, Roll No. 75, of Hominy, Oklahoma, being of sound and disposing mind and memory, publish and decree this my last

165

will and testament, hereby revoking all former wills by me made, this is to say;

1. I direct the payment of my last illness and funeral expenses as soon as possible.

2. I give and bequeath to John Abbott Roll No. 694 the following property, to-wit; All the estate inherited by me from the estate Ah-sin-kah Roll No. 720 (which includes about 656 acres of land $1900.00 Trust Funds, and Oil and gas royalty) and $1000.00 of my Trust funds, said land in Osage County, Oklahoma.

3. I give and bequeath to Me-ke-wah-ti-an-kah, Roll No. 52, the following property, to-wit; My second selection of land (known as my second allotment and consist of 160 acres of land) in Osage County, Oklahoma, and $500.00 of my Trust Funds.

4. I give and bequeath to my husband Shun-kah-mo-lah, Roll No. 74 the following property, to-wit; My homestead (W1/2 of SE1/4, and NE1/4 of SW1/4, and SW1/4 of NE1/4 of Sec 12, Twp. 22, Range 8) and my third and fourth selection of land in Osage County, Oklahoma and $1500.00 of my Trust Funds, my Oil and Gas royalty and all the rest and residue of my property, real and personal of whatever kind, and wherever situated.

Witness my hand this the *3rd* day of July, 1915, I have signed my last will and testament (my mark) consisting of two sheets of paper.

	her
Witnesses to Mark,	*Wah-tsa-me* [thumb print]
Prentiss Price	*mark*
Wiley G Haines	

Wah-tsa-me, Osage Allottee No. 75, being unable to sign her name to the attached and foregoing instrument, she requested me, the undersigned **Prentiss Price** to sign her name thereto in her behalf, which I thereupon did in the presence of Wah-tsa-me, Roll No. 75, and in the presence of the said Prentiss Price and **Wiley G Haines** and thereupon Wah-tsa-me, Roll No. 75 made her mark to said signature by me made, and declared and published the above and foregoing instrument, as her last will and testament, and requested the undersigned witnesses to sign their names thereto as witnesses, which they did in her presence and in the presence of one another, on the *3rd* day of July, 1915.

Indian Wills, 1911 – 1921 Book Three
Records of The Bureau of Indian Affairs

Prentiss Price   P.O. Hominy, Okla.
Wiley G Haines   P.O. Hominy, Okla.
Charles Grant   P.O. Hominy, Okla.

I, *Chas Grant* do hereby certify that before the execution of the foregoing will, I correctly and fully translated its contents to said testatrix and that she knew and understood the contents of the same.

Charles Grant
Interpreter.

Department of The Interior,
Office of Indian Affairs, Washington,

JUN -2 1916

It is respectfully recommended that the within will be approved in pursuance of the Act of April 18, 1912 (37 Stat. L., 86, 88).

Respectfully,
EB Meritt
Assistant Commissioner.

Department of The Interior
Office of The Secretary   JUN 3- 1916

The within will is hereby approved in pursuance of the provisions of the Act of April 18, 1912 (37 Stat. L., 86, 88).

Bo Sweeney
Assistant Secretary

▲▼▲▼▲▼▲▼▲▼▲▼▲▼▲▼
TWIN or WA-RA-CHA-NA-KAW

LAST WILL AND TESTAMENT OF

TWIN or WA-RA-CHA-NA-KAW
Winnebago Agency, Nebr.,
June 2, 1915.

I, Twin or Wa-ra-cha-na-kaw, Winnebago allottee No. 732, being in my right mind and of disposing memory and realizing that I must soon pass away, make this my last will and testament, uninfluened[sic] by any persons or stress of circumstances.

To my son Jacob Twin I give and bequeath the Southwest quarter of the Northeast quarter of Section thirty-four, Township twenty-seven North of Range 7, East of the Sixth Principal Meridian, Nebr.

To Mary Twin, my daughter, I give and bequeath the Southeast quarter of the Northeast quarter of Section thirty-four, Township twenty-seven North, Range seven East of the Sixth Principal Meridian, Nebraska.

To my son Louis Twin I give and bequeath the Southwest quarter of the Northwest quarter of Section fourteen, Township twenty-six North, Range nine East of the Sixth Principal Meridian, Nebraska.

To James Joseph Twin and Rufus A. Twin, my sons, I give and bequeath all funds which may be to my credit with the Superintendent or other officer in Charge of the Winnebago Reservation at the time of my death, after all funeral expenses and just debts have been paid, such debts before payment to receive the approval of the Superintendent or other Officer in Charge of the Winnebago Reservation. To James Joseph Twin and Rufus A. Twin I also give and bequeath my interest in allotment No. 570 of Chump-ah-ka-ra-che-win-kaw, my deceased mother, this interest, I understand, being one-seventh, the allotment of my mother being described as the Southwest quarter of the Northwest quarter and the Northwest quarter of the Northwest quarter of Section seventeen, Township twenty-six North, Range seven East of the Sixth Principal Meridian, Nebraska, and the N.W. 1/4 of the S.E. 1/4, Sec. 15, T. 26 N., R. 9 E. 6th P.M., Neb.

I am aware that in this Will I have favored Mary Twin and Jacob Twin. I do this for the reason that Mary Twin has taken care of me and Jacob Twin is my only son raising a family. I am also aware that the land I am Willing to Louis Twin is not as valuable as that which I am Willing to Mary and Jacob.

At my request, Fred A. Gross and Karl W. Greene are signing as witnesses to this Will in my presence and I am signing in their presence, all signing in the presence of each other.

His

Witnesses: Twin or Warachanakaw [thumb print]
F. A. Gross
Karl W Greene

Indian Wills, 1911 – 1921 Book Three
Records of The Bureau of Indian Affairs

We, Fred A. Gross and Karl W. Greene, have witnesses the signing of the above Will and Testament by Twin or Warachanakaw, signing in his presence at his request, all the three parties signing in the presence of each other.

F.A Gross
Karl W. Greene

I, Frank T. Thunder, hereby certify that I interpreted for Twin or Warachanakaw and that the above instrument represents his true Will and Testament.

Frank T. Thunder

Department of The Interior,
Office of Indian Affairs, Washington,
JUN -2 1916

It is recommended that the within will be approved pursuant to the provisions of the Act of June 25, 1910 (36 Stats. L., 855-6) as amended by Act of February 14, 1913 (37 Stats. L., 678).

EB Meritt
Assistant Commissioner

Department of The Interior
Office of The Secretary JUN -3 1916

The within will of Twin (or Wa-ra-cha-na-kaw) is hereby approved pursuant to the provisions of the Act of June 25, 1910 (36 Stats. L., 855-6) as amended by Act of February 14, 1913 (37 Stats. L., 678).

Bo Sweeney
Assistant Secretary

▲▼▲▼▲▼▲▼▲▼▲▼▲▼

HARD WOMAN

Copy of will of Hard Woman.

Allen, So. Dak.,
April 5, 1914.

Le makiyuta pi kin he Sam H. Hawk 160 acre waqu we. Na 160 Mrs. Three Bear waqu we na maza ska tona akob iyaye kin hena akiye na na yuhapi kte.

169

Indian Wills, 1911 – 1921 Book Three
Records of The Bureau of Indian Affairs

Hard Woman   x

Sutawin.

Waayatabub,

Lucy Red Nest, Howard Red Bear, Jessie Red Bear, Lucy Arapahoe.

Interpreted by Peter Chief Eagle, Special police.

Allen, So. Dak.,
April 5, 1914.

Tha land I give Sam H. Hawk 160 acres and Mrs. Three Bear 160 acres, and the money that is left over I want all of them to have equal parts.

Hard Woman   x

Sutawin (Indian for Hard Woman)

Witnesses:

Lucy Red Nest. Howard Red Bear.
Jessie Red Bear. Lucy Arapahoe.

Department of The Interior,
Office of Indian Affairs, Washington,
APR 17 1916

It is recommended that the within will be dis-approved in accordance with the Act of June 25, 1910 (36 Stats. L., 855-6) as amended by Act of February 14, 1913 (37 Stats. L., 678).

Respectfully
EB Meritt
Assistant Commissioner

Department of The Interior
Office of The Secretary MAY 20 1916

The within will is hereby ----approved in accordance with the Act of June 25, 1910 (36 Stats. L., 855-6) as amended by Act of February 14, 1913 (37 Stats. L., 678).

Indian Wills, 1911 – 1921 Book Three
Records of The Bureau of Indian Affairs

Bo Sweeney
Assistant Secretary

Department of The Interior,
Office of Indian Affairs, Washington,
MAY 19 1916

It is recommended that the within will be approved in accordance with the Act of June 25, 1910 (36 Stats. L., 855-6) as amended by Act of February 14, 1913 (37 Stats. L., 678).

Respectfully
CF Hawke
Acting Assistant Commissioner

▲▼▲▼▲▼▲▼▲▼▲▼▲▼▲▼

KILLS AT NIGHT

Original
WILL

OFFICE OF INDIAN AFFAIRS
RECEIVED
APR 8 1916
38567

I, **Kills At Night** of Pine Ridge Agency, South Dakota, Allottee number **3075** do hereby make and declare this to be my last will and testament, in accordance with Section 2 of the Act of June 25, 1910, (36 stat. 855-858) and Act of February 14, 1913, (Public No. 381), hereby revoking all former wills made by me:

1. I hereby direct that as soon as possible after my decease, that all my debts, funeral and testamentary expenses be paid out of my personal estate.

2. I give and devise my allotment on the Pine Ridge Reservation, South Dakota, described as follows:

N1/2 of Section 32, P N1/2 of Section 33, Township 37 N., R. 46 W of 6th P.M. in South Dakota, containing 640 acres.

in the following manner:

To my daughter Nellie Fast the N.W.1/4 of Sec. 32

To " sister Louisa No Water, N.E.1/4 "   "   "

171

Indian Wills, 1911 – 1921 Book Three
Records of The Bureau of Indian Affairs

To " Brother Homer Iron Hawk, N.W.1/4 of Sec. 33.

To " wife Annie Kills at Night, N.E.1/4 of Sec. 33, all in Township 37 N., R. 46 W. of the 6th P.M. in South Dakota.

3. I give and bequeath all of my personal property of whatsoever nature and wheresoever situated unto

One gray horse branded (Blank) **saddle and bridal to my brother Homer Iron Hawk.**

Two gentle mares, one gray and one pinto; to my wife Annie Kills At Night.

4. All the rest of my property, real or personal, now possessed or hereafter acquired, of whatsoever nature and wheresoever situated, I hereby give, devise and bequeath unto

To my brother Homer Iron Hawk all of my farming implements

To my brother Homer Iron Hawk One house unfinished.

House, corrals and fences, to my wife Annie Kills At Night,

To my wife all of my cattle

In witness whereof I have hereunto set my hand this *8th* day of *October* 1915

WITNESSES TO SIGNATURE BY MARK.

Leonard L Smith	*his*
Farmer, Oglala, S.D.	*Kills At Night* [thumb print]
Mark R. Eagle	*mark*
Ass't Farmer, Oglala, S.D.	

The above statement was, this **8th** day of **October** 1915 signed and published by **Kills At Night** as **his** last will and testament, in the joint presence of the undersigned, the said **Kills At Night** then being of sound and vigorous mid and free from any constraint or compulsion; whereupon we, being without any interest in the matter other than friendship, and being well acquainted with **him** but not members of **his** family, immediately subscribed our names hereto in the presence of each other and of the said testator, for the purpose of attesting the said will, as **he** requested us to do. And that I, **L.L. Smith** at the testator's request, have written **his** name in ink, and that **I** affixed **his** thumb-mark.

		Post Office Address
Leonard L Smith	**Farmer,**	**Oglala, S. D.**
Mark R Eagle	**Ass't Farmer**	" "

Pine Ridge, South Dakota.
Apr -4 1916

I hereby certify that I have fully inquired into the mental competency of the Indian signing the above will; the circumstances attending the execution of the will; the influence that may have induced its execution, and the names of those entitled to share in the estate under the law of descent in South Dakota: reasons for the disposition of the property proposed by the will differing from disposition had the property descended by operation of law.

I respectfully forward this will with the recommendation that it be …..approved.

John R Brennan
Supt. & Spl. Disb. Agent.

Department of The Interior,
Office of Indian Affairs, Washington,
MAY 16 1916

It is recommended that the within will be approved in accordance with the Act of June 25, 1910 (36 Stats. L., 855-6) as amended by Act of February 14, 1913 (37 Stats. L., 678).

Respectfully,
CF Hawke
Acting Assistant Commissioner

Department of The Interior
Office of The Secretary
MAY 18 1916

The within will is hereby approved in accordance with the Act of June 25, 1910 (36 Stats. L., 855-6) as amended by Act of February 14, 1913 (37 Stats. L., 678).

Bo Sweeney
Assistant Secretary

Indian Wills, 1911 – 1921 Book Three
Records of The Bureau of Indian Affairs

▲▼▲▼▲▼▲▼▲▼▲▼▲▼▲▼

THERESA MORGAN BLACKBIRD

Last Will and Testament of Theresa Morgan Blackbird.

I, Theresa Morgan Blackbird, being of sound and disposing mind and memory and being in full possession of my mental faculties and and[sic] having clearly in mind the extent, value condition of my property real, and personal, and knowing my issue and natural and legal heirs and the claims of each of them upon my bounty, do hereby and by these presents following, make and publish this my last will and testament, in words following:

First:

All moneys, loans and credits which I may have at the time of my death, I desire disposed of as follows: it is my will that my administrator, hereinafter names use sufficient thereof under order of the Court to build a suitable house on the South half of the northeast quarter of Sec. 20, twp. 25, R. 10, which I own: and I give, and bequeath unto the issue of my brother Alfred Hallowell, who may survive me, $100.00, share and share alike; the remainder of such moneys and funds I give and bequeath unto my four children, Albert, Eliza, Frank, and Nellie, share and share alike.

Second:

I give and bequeath unto my daughter, Nellie W. McCaulley, my three horses; and any and all other personal property which I may have at the time of my death, which is not disposed of in the first paragraph above, I give and bequeath unto my said four children share and share alike.

Third:

The south half of the northeast quarter of sec. 20, twp. 25, R. 10, in Thurston County, Nebraska, which I own in fee simple, I give, devise and bequeath unto my four children Albert Morgan, Eliza Morgan Thomas, Frank Blackbird and Nellie Webster McCaulley, share and share alike.

174

Fourth:

I give and devise unto my daughter Nellie Webster McCaulley the southwest quarter of the northeast quarter of sec. 32, twp. 25, R. 7, being the allotment of Hutata Hallowell which I own under restrictions, provided however if the said Nellie Webster McCaulley shall have no issue which shall survive her, then and in that event, it is my will that the remainder fee title to said premises shall pass to my other issue who may survive her but if she shall have issue surviving her then said premises shall pass to such surviving issue.

Fifth:

I give, devise and bequeath unto my said four children Albert, Eliza, Frank and Nellie the interest and share which I may own in the southeast quarter of the northeast quarter of sec. 4, twp. 24, R. 7, share and share alike.

Sixth:

If any of my property real and personal or otherwise should be held under restrictions of trust patent of allotment at the time of my death, I request the Hon. Sec. of the Interior to approve the above will and at the proper time to issue patents in fee therefore subject to and in accordance with the terms of the above will.

Seventh:

I hereby revoke any former will that I may have made.

Eighth:

I hereby appoint Harry L. Keefe the executor of this my last will and testament subject to his acceptance thereof and furnishing the bonds as provided by law.

In witness whereof I have hereunto set my hand and do hereby declare the above instrument to be my last will and testament this 11th day of December, 1913.   her
                                         Theresa Morgan Blackbird,
In the presence of   thumbmark

Silas Hallowell
Jeanette Hallowell.

We, the undersigned do hereby certify that the above testatrix
signed the above last will and testament after the same had been carefully
and correctly read over to her and explained to her in the indian[sic]
language and when she signed the same with her thumb mark she
declared in our presence and in the presence of each of us that the above
was her last will and testament; that she understood it; that it was exactly
as she wanted it and we, at her request and in her presence and in the
presence of each other signed the same as subscribing witnesses all on
this 11th day of December, 1913.

Silas Hallowell
Jeanette Hallowell.

State of Nebraska,)
) ss.
Thurston County   )

I, Roy B. Carlberg, County Judge of Thurston County,
Nebraska, do hereby certify that the within and foregoing is a true and
correct copy of the last will and testament of Theresa Morgan Blackbird
as the same appears on file and of record in the County Court of Thurston
County, Nebraska, and that the same was duly admitted to probate,
proven and allowed as the last will and testament of the said Theresa
Morgan Blackbird by Frank Flynn, County Judge of said Thurston
County, Nebraska, on the 8th day of June, 1914.

Roy B. Carlberg
County Judge.

Department of The Interior,
Office of Indian Affairs, Washington,
MAY 17 1916
It is recommended that the within certified copy be approved according to
the Act of June 25, 1910 (36 Stats. L., 855-6) as amended by Act of
February 14, 1913 (37 Stats. L., 678), so far as it relates to the trust
property of the testatrix.

Respectfully,
CF Hawke
Acting Assistant Commissioner.

Indian Wills, 1911 – 1921 Book Three
Records of The Bureau of Indian Affairs

Department of The Interior
Office of The Secretary MAY 18 1916

The within certified copy is hereby approved according to the Act of June 25, 1910 (36 Stats. L., 855-6) as amended by Act of February 14, 1913 (37 Stats. L., 678), so far as it relates to the trust property of the testatrix.

Bo Sweeney
Assistant Secretary

▲▼▲▼▲▼▲▼▲▼▲▼▲▼▲▼

STRIKES AMONG THE CROWD

WILL AND LAST TESTAMENT OF STRIKES AMONG THE CROWD.
Wife of Arm Around The Neck.

I, Strikes Among The Crowd, wife of Arm Around The Neck, of Lodge Grass, Montana, declare this my last will and testament.

I will and bequeath unto Barney One Goose,
One black gelding horse, 2 yrs old, branded RM
One sorrell filley[sic] horse, 1 yrs old, branded RM
One sixth (1/6) interest and share of all my real estate, after the death of my husband the share and interest is to be one third (1/3),

I will and bequeath unto Medicine Tail, wife of Left Hand
One sixth (1/6) interest and share of all my real estate, after the death of my husband the share and interest is to be one third (1/3),

I will and bequeath unto One Star,
One grey gelding horse, 5 yrs old, branded RM
One sorrel gelding horse, 1 yr old, branded RM
One sixth (1/6) interest and share of all my real estate, after the death of my husband the share and interest is to be one third (1/3),

I will and bequeath unto my husband, Arm Around The Neck,
All of my personal estate not mentioned in the above,
One half (1/2) interest and share of all my real estate.

Strikes Among the
Crowd, her thumb   [thumb print]
mark.

Signed, sealed, published and declared by the above Strikes Among The Crowd, wife of Arm Around The Neck, as and for her last will and testament, in the presence of us, who have hereunto subscribed our names at her request as witnesses thereto, in the presence of said testator, and of each other.

John F Hargrave   Farmer, Lodge Grass, Montana.
George Hill   Govt. Interpreter, Lodge Grass, Mont.

Subscribed and sworn to before me this 23rd day of January, 1915.
William A. Petzoldt,
Notary Public,   *William A. Petzoldt*
Lodge Grass, Montana
My commission expires Jan 29th. 1916

Department of The Interior,
Office of Indian Affairs, Washington,
MAY 10 1916

The within will of Strikes In A (Among The) Crowd is recommended for approval in accordance with the Act of June 25, 1910 (36 Stats. L., 855-6) as amended by Act of February 14, 1913 (37 Stats. L., 678).

Respectfully
CF Hawke
Acting Assistant Commissioner

Department of The Interior
Office of The Secretary MAY 10 1916

The within will is hereby approved under the Act of June 25, 1910 (36 Stats. L., 855-6) as amended by Act of February 14, 1913 (37 Stats. L., 678).

Bo Sweeney
Assistant Secretary

▲ ▼ ▲ ▼ ▲ ▼ ▲ ▼ ▲ ▼ ▲ ▼ ▲ ▼

<u>**JOHN HALFIRON**</u>

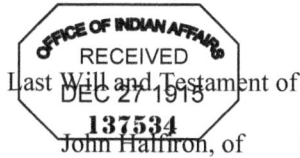

Last Will and Testament of

John Halfiron, of

OFFICE OF INDIAN AFFAIRS
RECEIVED
DEC 27 1915
137534

Santee, Neb.

OFFICE OF INDIAN AFFAIRS
RECEIVED
JUN 2 1913
68606

I, John Halfiron, of Santee, Nebraska, do hereby make, publish and declare this my last will and testament in words and figures as follows:

I give and devise unto my only daughter, Lucy Westerman, all of my personal property, funds to my credit in the Office of the Superintendent of the Santee Reservation and my allotment consisting of the East Half of the South West quarter of Section 12, Township 32 north, Range four west of the 6th P.M. in Knox County, Nebraska, after all necessary funeral expenses shall have been paid. Signed this 29th day of May, 1913.

his thumb

John Halfiron [thumb print]

mark

Witnesses to signature by
Mark: *Robert Brown*
Lot Frazier

We, whose names are hereunto subscribed do hereby certify that John Halfiron, the testator, subscribed his name to this instrument in our presence, and in the presence of each of us, and declared at the same time, in our presence and hearing, that this instrument was his last will and testament, and we, at his request, sign our names hereto in his presence as witnesses this *29th* day of May, 1913.

Robert Brown
Lot Frazier

Department of The Interior,
Office of Indian Affairs, Washington,

NOV -5 1913

It is recommended that the within will be approved pursuant to the provisions of the Act of February 14, 1913 (37 Stats. 678).

Respectfully,
CF Hawke
Second Assistant Commissioner.

Indian Wills, 1911 – 1921 Book Three
Records of The Bureau of Indian Affairs

Department of The Interior
Office of The Secretary NOV -6 1913

The within will approved pursuant to the provisions of the Act of February 14, 1913 (37 Stats. 678).

Bo Sweeney
Assistant Secretary

▲ ▼ ▲ ▼ ▲ ▼ ▲ ▼ ▲ ▼ ▲ ▼ ▲ ▼ ▲ ▼

Index

Index

www.ingramcontent.com/pod-product-compliance
Lightning Source LLC
Chambersburg PA
CBHW030245030426

42336CB00009B/256